MICROWAVES PROPERLY EXPLAINED

To Huw, Emma and Lindsay
with thanks for their honest opinions
and their continued encouragement.

MICROWAVE
COOKING
PROPERLY
EXPLAINED

WITH RECIPES

Annette Yates

RIGHT WAY

Constable & Robinson Ltd
3 The Lanchesters
162 Fulham Palace Road
London W6 9ER
www.constablerobinson.com

First published in the UK in 1979.
This new revised edition published by Right Way,
an imprint of Constable & Robinson, 2010

A copy of the British Library Cataloguing in
Publication Data is available from the British Library

ISBN: 978-0-7160-2238-1

Printed and bound in the EU

3   5   7   9   10   8   6   4   2

CONTENTS

ACKNOWLEDGEMENTS

I could not have written this book without the help and kindness of many people – the Microwave Technologies Association and their members, several microwave manufacturers, makers and suppliers of microwave cookware and my home economics colleagues in the microwave industry – all of whom have generously shared their expertise with me. My thanks go to each and every one.

INTRODUCTION

I welcomed the opportunity to update this book. On reading the original text I soon realised that during the writing of it I had been more than a little guilty of treating the microwave as the ultimate answer to all cooking. Over the years my attitude has matured and I now see the microwave oven not as an isolated appliance but as a valuable part of the kitchen team. Today, my microwave works hand in hand with the hob, the grill, the toaster, the kettle and, sometimes, the conventional oven. No longer am I prepared to cook foods in the microwave oven simply 'because you can'. If I cannot get the best results, I use a better method. As a consequence, many of the old recipes have been replaced by new ones – recipes which have been tried and tested by family and friends and which have cooked successfully in a variety of microwave ovens. You will notice too that many of the recipes make use of a variety of microwave power levels – to get the best results every time.

I avoid cooking complicated courses with several accompaniments – there is a danger of spending longer in the kitchen than bargained for, and, much as I love cooking, I too seem to have less and less time to divide between my responsibilities. Instead, I prefer to cook some parts of the meal in the microwave while simultaneously cooking the rest on the hob or under the grill. This is my route to the largest time savings and superior meals.

This book is all about fitting a microwave into your life, not about fitting your life around a microwave. If you have recently acquired your first microwave oven, try not to be too hard on yourself. The best way to gain confidence is to take one step at a time, using the microwave to cook one part of each meal. It will soon earn its keep, once you have had the time to get to know it and the foods it cooks best for *you*. In no time at all, you will wonder how you ever managed without it.

To those of you who are already confident with your microwave oven, I hope you will pick up more handy tips and enjoy the recipes, many of which are new to the book.

Happy microwaving!

Annette Yates

1

ADVANTAGES AND LIMITATIONS

Before buying a microwave, you need to know how it will benefit you and what it is capable of achieving.

What are the advantages of microwave cooking?
- Cooking times are much shorter. Conventional cooking times can be cut by as much as 60–75 per cent.

- Food can be thawed quickly using a microwave.

- It's economical. A microwave uses about 25 per cent of the power needed to run a conventional oven (a combination oven uses a little more). Added to this, cooking times are shorter and, when you make full use of a microwave, the lower the power level used, the lower the electricity consumption.

- It's versatile. Most foods can be thawed, cooked and reheated in a microwave.

- It's convenient. Snacks and meals can be prepared as and when they are needed. A microwave copes particularly well with small quantities and single portions, and in households where individuals eat at different times, a microwave is a boon.

• It's easy to use. A microwave can be plugged in anywhere there is 13 amp socket. Controls are generally straightforward to use. Oven cleaning is minimal too.

• It saves on washing up, because many foods can be cooked in their serving dishes.

• Microwaves are clean and cool, and are particularly suitable for use by elderly and disabled people and children.

• Low-fat and fat-free cooking is easy with a microwave.

• Flavour and nutritive value are excellent in foods cooked in a microwave. Many foods can be cooked simply in their own juices; others with just a little additional liquid. Cooking foods for the briefest time, and in the least liquid, is known to be one of the best ways to retain maximum food value.

Is there anything a microwave can't do?
• Browning and crisping are not possible unless the microwave oven has a grill or it is a combination oven (see page 20).

• Frying, either in shallow or deep fat, is not possible.

• It cannot successfully cook eggs in their shells.

• A microwave cannot make toast, unless it incorporates an efficient grill.

• It cannot make pancakes.

- A microwave cannot cook crusty pastry and bread, foods in batter, Yorkshire pudding, roast potatoes or soufflés, unless it is a combination oven (see page 20).

- Heating more than 300 ml (½ pint) water is more economical in an electric kettle.

- A microwave cannot speed up the cooking of some foods. Rice, pasta and pulses, for example, generally take as long to cook in the microwave as they do conventionally.

To sum up
- A microwave oven is invaluable when used, not as an isolated appliance, but as part of the team of cooking equipment in the kitchen. Used together with the hob, grill, kettle, toaster and conventional oven, a microwave oven will help you to get the best results in the shortest time.

2

THE MICROWAVE

What are microwaves and how do they cook food?
Cooking with microwaves is quite different from conventional methods which use electricity, gas or solid fuel. In a conventional oven the walls and the air inside them are heated first. As the oven heats up, so does the surface of the food. This surface heat, in turn, is slowly conducted to the centre of the food.

In a microwave oven the walls and air are not heated. The microwaves pass straight into the food, to heat it directly.

Microwaves are electromagnetic waves, similar to radio and television waves. Electric energy is converted into microwaves by a valve called a magnetron. The microwaves are channelled along a wave guide, then a stirrer or paddle distributes them evenly into the oven cavity. Once they are inside the oven, three things happen to the microwaves.

1. They are *reflected* off the metal walls and bounce around inside the oven cavity.

2. They are *transmitted* by glass, china, pottery, microwave plastics and paper. So the microwaves pass straight through dishes made of these materials.

3. They are *absorbed* by water (in particular) in food. When the water molecules absorb microwave energy they become agitated and vibrate at an incredible speed – about 2,450 million times per second! It is this excitement which generates the heat which, in turn, cooks the food in a very short time. Microwaves can only penetrate food about 4 cm (1½ inches), so anything thicker than 8 cm (3 inches) relies on heat from the outer areas being conducted to the centre – just like conventional cooking.

Fig. 1. The metal walls of the oven reflect the microwaves.
(Food is not shown in the oven for the purposes of this diagram, but, remember, a microwave oven should never be switched on empty.)

Fig. 2. Certain cooking containers transmit microwaves.

Fig. 3. Food absorbs microwaves and heats up.

Are microwaves safe?

- Microwaves produce a change in temperature only. They should not be confused with X-rays.

- Microwaves cannot be produced unless the oven door is securely closed. The doors and hinges are fitted with locks, seals and cut-out switches which automatically switch off the microwaves the instant the door is opened.

- The mesh in the oven door allows the cook to see inside the oven, but the holes in this mesh are not large enough to allow the microwaves to escape. They simply bounce off the mesh back into the oven cavity.

- British safety standards regarding leakage of microwave ovens are extremely strict. Ovens are built to precise specifications and they are thoroughly tested before leaving the factory. When buying a microwave oven, look for the BEAB (British Electrotechnical Approvals Board) label for household appliances, which means that a microwave oven has met safety requirements dictated by the relevant British Standard Specification for electrical safety and microwave leakage limits.

Fig. 4. The main parts of a microwave oven

1. Lead from oven to 13 amp plug.
2. Door fastening. There may be two or more locking devices to ensure that microwaves are switched off as soon as the door is opened.
3. Removable shelf or turntable. This raises the food off the oven floor, so that microwaves can be absorbed from underneath too. It makes the job of mopping up spilled food easier and it also ensures that the food is in the best position to receive the microwaves (with a turn table, the food is carried around the oven to ensure even absorption of microwaves).
4. Interior light. This usually lights as soon as the oven is switched on.
5. Controls. Basic controls include an on/off button, a timer control and a control to adjust the microwave power level.
6. Door stop.

3

CHOOSING A
MICROWAVE OVEN

Choosing a microwave oven is an exciting experience, so long as you are not intimidated by the vast choice on offer today. This section lists some of the questions worth answering before buying. It then goes on to outline many of the features on offer today. Whether you are buying your first microwave or you are updating your current model, I hope to help you choose one which will fit in with the way you cook and eat.

How much do you want to spend?
Though price may dictate your choice initially, deciding which features you would like on an oven will also help to narrow down a price band.

How much space do you have and where?
Will the microwave sit on the kitchen work surface or on a shelf or brackets, or will you want it built into the kitchen? Do you wish to move it around, perhaps on self-catering holidays? Remember it needs to be close to a 13 amp socket. Most ovens need ventilation, so check you will be able to leave a space all round yours. Position the oven so that you have a small area of work surface next to it – for taking dishes out of the microwave and setting them down.

Will your microwaving be restricted to thawing and reheating?

If so, a basic model will be sufficient – a low wattage oven with cooking, heating and defrost settings. If, however, you will want to make full use of the microwave oven and cook all the things it does well – soups, snacks, sauces, fish, vegetables, poultry, casseroles, fruit and puddings – you will need at least 600W and several power levels (see page 18).

How many do you cook for?

Check the inside of the microwave oven. Is it large enough to take your largest casserole dish, or the largest item you are likely to cook? Will your dishes fit, and turn round, on the turntable? Even if you cook for one or two people most of the time, are you likely to cook for large numbers in the future?

Do you already have an efficient grill?

If not, you may consider buying a microwave oven which incorporates a grill (see page 20).

Do you regularly cook roast meals, pastry, cakes or oven-cooked food coated in breadcrumbs or batter?

If so, you may consider buying a combination oven (see page 20) which combines the heat of a traditional oven with microwave cooking.

FEATURES ON MICROWAVE AND COMBINATION OVENS

Controls can be mechanical or touch-control. Both are easy to use, but for accurate timing in seconds (for softening butter, for instance) choose a digital display. Touch-control panels are easy to wipe clean.

Oven interiors can be stainless steel or plastic-coated. Both are easy to clean, and personal preference will dictate which you choose. Combination ovens (see page 20) often have at least one self-clean lining; some top-of-the-range models have a pyrolytic cleaning function – the oven can be heated to a temperature which is high enough to burn off any food residue.

A *turntable* helps food to cook evenly by raising it off the oven floor so the microwaves can reach underneath, and by turning the food as it cooks. When buying a microwave with a turntable, check that your cooking containers and plates are not so large that they prevent the turntable turning.

Wave stirrers or paddles (which are concealed) also encourage even cooking by distributing the microwaves evenly into the oven cavity. Some ovens have both a turntable and wave stirrers.

Power output indicates the amount of microwave energy used to cook food. It ranges from 500W to 1000W. The higher the wattage (W), the faster the microwave cooks. Recipes in magazines and books use differently powered ovens so read the instructions carefully. Recipes in this book use 750–850W. Cooking times on many pre-packed foods are generally based on 650–800W, and 750–850W, just look at the packet. If you are using a more powerful oven, you will need either to reduce the cooking time or lower the power level and cook for the normal time. If your microwave oven has less power, cook a little longer.

Power levels control the amount of microwave energy entering the oven, so food can be cooked as quickly or as slowly as you like. Manufacturers vary in the way they describe power levels – some have up to nine settings but the most useful are HIGH (100%), MEDIUM-HIGH (75%), MEDIUM (50%), MEDIUM-LOW (30%) and LOW (10%).

A *shelf* allows more food to be cooked at the same time,

though cooking times will be longer. The same amount of microwave energy goes into the oven, no matter how much food it holds, and this energy has to be shared out.

An *auto-minute* button is handy. Just press it to cook for 1 minute on HIGH (100%).

Quick/Rapid/Jet start or *Boost* is designed for quick heating of liquids and drinks in particular. It usually works on a higher power than that used for everyday cooking.

A *minute timer* or alarm can sometimes be used as an automatic timer, with no cooking involved.

Auto-defrost is a useful feature, though most foods can be thawed on DEFROST or MEDIUM-LOW (30%). Auto-defrost is controlled either by time or by the weight of the food. Some models have a sensor which weighs the food and automatically calculates the thawing time.

Auto cook/heat allows you to program in the type of food and its weight, then the oven does the rest – calculating the cooking time, appropriate power levels and, in combination ovens, the temperature. Some models have an automatic sensing device which does this. This auto-cook/heat feature is particularly useful for large pieces of meat and for ready meals.

Hold-warm puts the oven on a low power level to keep food warm for 15 minutes or more.

Multi-sequence cooking allows you to program the oven to cook on a series of cooking times and power levels – for example, cooking on HIGH (100%) for a set time, switching to MEDIUM (50%) for a set time, then holding on LOW (10%) for a time.

Auto-repeat recalls the last program used.

A *memory* function stores programs – useful only if you cook the same dishes frequently

Delay-start/Pre-set/Auto-start delays cooking for several hours, if necessary, perhaps while you are out. This feature is more useful in a combination oven (for conventional or combination cooking) than in a microwave where cooking times are very short anyway and may need turning or stirring.

A *grill* is useful for improving the appearance of microwaved food, and if you do not already have an efficient conventional grill. Don't expect a grill in a microwave oven to be as powerful as a conventional grill, though, and it is likely to operate only with the door closed. Some ovens allow simultaneous grilling and microwaving to save time. Grills with radiant elements are similar to conventional electric grills. Halogen bulbs give instant heat, though they are usually restricted to only one area of the oven ceiling. A quartz grill is both quick and efficient.

A *combination oven* combines the speed of microwaving with the traditional heat of a conventional oven. Foods can be browned and crisped as well as cooked in a fraction of the usual time. A combination oven is particularly useful if you regularly cook whole poultry and meat joints, pastry, cakes, Yorkshire pudding, soufflés and other foods which need a crisp and brown finish.

As the name suggests, a combination oven can be used in three ways: on microwave only, on convection only (using traditional heat in °C), or with a combination of the two (often called 'combination', 'dual-cook' or 'Hi-speed'). It is when cooking on 'combination' that models vary in the way they work. There are three main types:

- Where both the temperature and the microwave power level can be controlled by you.

- Where the temperature can be controlled, while the microwave power level is pre-set.

- Where there are a series of pre-set programs in which specific temperatures are already matched up with selected microwave power levels.

Your choice will depend on whether you are a keen cook who likes to experiment, and who prefers to be able to adjust temperature and microwave power in order to achieve the results you want; or whether you prefer to have it all selected for you, ready simply to press a button.

Rotisserie units feature in some combination ovens, for cooking meat and poultry on a spit, using a combination of microwaving, grilling and convected heat.

An extra word on choice
When making your final choice, it is worth asking to see the instruction books and cook books which accompany the ovens. Some are better than others.

Microwave labels
A voluntary labelling scheme for microwave ovens and food packs was introduced in 1992. It was developed by the Ministry of Agriculture, Fisheries and Food (MAFF) in partnership with oven manufacturers, food manufacturers, retailers and consumer organisations. It is designed to help us to microwave food more successfully, particularly when heating small quantities of food, such as ready meals for one or two.
    New microwave ovens are now labelled with:

- The power output of the oven, based on an internationally agreed standard (IEC 705)

- A heating category letter, from A to E, to indicate the oven's ability to heat small food packs.

Fig. 5. The microwave labelling scheme.
1. Microwave symbol.
2. Power output (watts).
3. Healing category for small packs.

Food packs which are suitable for microwaving are marked with the microwave symbol plus appropriate heating category letters and cooking times. Then, you simply match up the information on the food pack with that on your microwave oven.

4

CONTAINERS FOR THE MICROWAVE

The containers which are suitable for microwave cooking are those which allow microwaves to pass straight through them into the food. You'll probably find that many of the dishes you already own will be fit for use in the microwave. Those which have their own lids are the most convenient.

What to use
Ovenglass, glass ceramic, china and some pottery are suitable. Although they let microwaves pass through them, you will still need to use oven gloves to lift them from the microwave oven, because the heat conducted from the food makes the dishes hot. Also, because they absorb a lot of heat from the food, cooking in these containers may take slightly longer than in materials which are specially designed for the microwave.

A wide range of microwave cookware is available today, not only in heat-resistant plastic, but also in oven glass and ceramic glass. The most versatile are suitable for microwave, conventional oven, freezer and dishwasher. They are usually fit for cooking foods which reach a very high temperature, such as those containing a high proportion of fat or sugar. Always check the labels before buying.

Paper, such as *absorbent kitchen paper, greaseproof paper and non-stick baking paper* should only be used for brief heating.

What not to use

Metal containers reflect microwaves and, in general, should not be used when microwaving.

Some microwave manufacturers suggest using small pieces of foil to shield food and prevent it overcooking – follow the instructions carefully. Others suggest cooking some foods in foil trays – do check with the instruction book and follow the method carefully. If the manufacturer of your oven does not advise it, don't do it – if anything were to go wrong, your guarantee would be affected.

Do not use plates or dishes which are decorated with gold, silver or metal paint. The microwaves will cause the metal to spark and blacken.

Avoid using unglazed or partly-glazed pottery, fine glass (it contains minute particles of metal), polystyrene, dairy product containers, and dishes which have been repaired with glue.

To test if a container is suitable for the microwave

Put the dish in the microwave oven and place a cup containing 150 ml (¼ pint) cold water inside it. Cook on HIGH (100%) for 1–2 minutes. The outer dish should remain cool while the water in the cup heats up. If the dish becomes warm, it has absorbed some of the microwaves and is unsuitable for use.

The shape matters

Circular containers are best because the microwaves reach the food equally from all sides. Though the centre usually cooks more slowly than the edges, stirring food during cooking encourages even results.

A *ring* shape produces best results and is particularly useful for foods which cannot be stirred – like cakes. There is no slow-cooking centre, so the food cooks evenly.

Squares and rectangles tend to overcook at their corners, where the microwaves are concentrated. They often have an area in the centre which cooks only slowly.

Straight sides on a container help the food to cook evenly. Sloping sides allow microwaves to concentrate in, and overcook, food at the outer edge.

Food wraps

Roasting bags and *microwave bags* are useful for microwave cooking. Follow the packet instructions for use. Ordinary polythene food bags are not suitable.

Cling film – It is not recommended that ordinary cling film is used. Look at the packaging to make sure it is suitable for use in the microwave. It can be used to cover dishes but do not allow it to touch the food. Pierce it, or turn back a small area, to allow steam to escape during cooking.

Absorbent kitchen paper, greaseproof paper and non-stick baking paper are useful for wrapping or covering foods.

Useful accessories

A *microwave rack* is handy to encourage even cooking of all foods – to raise dishes in the oven so that the microwaves can easily reach the food from every direction. They are also useful for thawing meat and other foods, preventing them from sitting in a pool of liquid.

Browning dishes are useful in microwave-only ovens. They have a special coating which heats up in the microwave, for searing and browning small items such as bacon, sausages, steaks, chops, eggs, fish, vegetables and toasted sandwiches. The surface of a browning dish can reach a temperature of up to 300°C (600°F). Always use oven gloves, follow the dish manufacturer's instructions carefully and never exceed the recommended pre-heating time. Once the food is put on to the hot sauce, cooking is completed by microwaving.

A *plate ring* is useful for stacking plated meals for thawing or reheating in the microwave. Best results are obtained if no more than two plates are stacked.

5

USING THE MICROWAVE

A microwave oven is a versatile piece of equipment which thaws, cooks and reheats food at a moment's notice. As you get to know your oven, you will discover that several things affect thawing/cooking/reheating times and the way the microwave performs generally:

• The type of food, its moisture content (the more it contains, the longer it takes to cook) and its density (dense foods like meat take longer to thaw than porous foods such as bread and cake).

• The quantity of food – two potatoes take longer to cook than one, though not necessarily double the time – for this reason, avoid filling the microwave with food.

• Its shape and size – regular shapes cook more evenly than irregular shapes, and small pieces cook quicker than large pieces.

• The starting temperature of the food dictates how long it takes to thaw/cook/reheat – for instance, food from the refrigerator takes longer to cook than food at room temperature.

- The container used – and its shape in particular – a circular shape with straight sides is best (see page 24).

- The power level used – the higher the power level, the faster the cooking.

- The way in which a food is cooked conventionally – food which normally requires slow, gentle cooking will benefit from cooking on a low power level in the microwave.

- The arrangement of the food – even layers encourage even heating; arrange individual foods in a circle with thicker areas towards the edge of the dish.

- Turning, stirring and repositioning foods encourages even results too.

- The standing time – most foods should be allowed to stand for a short time after microwaving – to allow the temperature to even out and to allow the food to finish thawing, cooking or reheating.

THAWING FOOD

A microwave and a freezer make a good partnership. Food which normally takes hours to thaw out can be taken from the freezer and thawed in the microwave in a matter of minutes.

Food is thawed using the DEFROST or MEDIUM-LOW (30%) setting. The food is subjected to microwave energy in short bursts for about 30% of the time period (in some ovens it is possible to hear the energy switching on and off as it pulsates into the oven). By controlling the microwave energy in this way, the food thaws slowly and evenly – during the periods when no microwaves are entering the oven, heat from the thawed areas is conducted to the colder areas. If the microwaves were not controlled, the food would thaw too quickly around the edges, heating up while the centre remained frozen solid.

After thawing, food should be allowed to stand for a short period, to allow any remaining ice crystals to disappear and to allow the temperature of the food to even out.

Many microwave ovens have an AUTO-DEFROST setting, which thaws food even more gently and incorporates a standing time too. Some models are controlled by time, during which the oven (which starts thawing on a fairly high power) gradually reduces the power level to LOW (10%). Some are controlled by the weight of the food – you simply program the oven with the type and weight of food to be thawed, and the oven does the rest. Others have a sensor which weighs the food and automatically calculates the thawing time.

Tips for thawing

• Frozen vegetables need no thawing – they can be cooked straight from the freezer.

• Containers which can be taken from freezer to microwave are the most convenient to use.

• Freeze food in shallow blocks – quick and even thawing.

• Put a block of frozen food into a close-fitting dish for thawing – to prevent thawed areas spreading over the base of the dish and heating up too soon.

• Before thawing, remove any excess ice which may be attached to food.

• Remove any metal ties, foil or foil containers before thawing.

• Open containers and bags of food before thawing – to prevent them splitting as the air inside heats and expands during thawing.

- Cover most food during thawing – to encourage even thawing in the minimum time. Baked foods, such as cakes, bread and pastries are best left uncovered – to prevent their surfaces from becoming too moist.

- Put cakes, bread and pastries on a sheet of absorbent kitchen paper – to soak up excess moisture during thawing.

- Arrange individual items in a circle, with the centre free, for even results.

- Follow the thawing times given in your oven manufacturer's instruction book until you are familiar with your oven.

- Turn and reposition large or dense foods at least once during thawing.

- Separate foods as they thaw (such as sausages, chops and fish fillets) to encourage even thawing. Break up blocks of food (such as sauces and soups) as they soften.

- Should any part of the food begin to feel warm, stop thawing and allow it to stand for several minutes before starting again.

Ensure poultry and meat are completely thawed before cooking.

REHEATING FOOD

Food reheats efficiently in a microwave, in a fraction of the time taken conventionally; and its colour, texture and flavour can be just as good as freshly-cooked food.

Tips for reheating
- The colder the food, the longer it will take to heat – food from the refrigerator takes longer than food at room temperature.

- Avoid reheating large, solid items, such as a joint of meat. Results are more successful if it is sliced first.

- Arrange food with care – in shallow, even layers. A plate of food should be arranged so that there is one even layer, with thick, dense items towards the edge.

- Two plated meals can be reheated by stacking one on top of the other, with a plate ring between them. Turn the plates (in opposite directions) at least once during reheating.

- Cover or wrap food during reheating – to retain heat and moisture so that it heats evenly and quickly. Bread, pastry, crumble toppings, and similar foods which need to be kept dry, should be reheated uncovered.

- Most foods can be reheated on HIGH (100%). Some are better on MEDIUM (50%) or MEDIUM-LOW (30%) such as bread; large casseroles and dishes like lasagne, moussaka and shepherd's pie; Christmas pudding; fruit; and mince pies.

- Stir foods whenever possible during reheating– such as soups, sauces, casseroles, milk puddings and drinks (see page 183). Turn or reposition large items at least once – such as poultry or meat pieces, whole potatoes, lasagne, moussaka and shepherd's pie.

- Always under-estimate reheating times to avoid overheating food. It is preferable to put the food back in the oven to heat for a little longer, rather than spoil it.

- Make sure that reheated food is *piping hot throughout*.

- Use a food thermometer if you want to make sure that the centre of the food is hot.

- Allow food to stand after reheating – to allow its temperature to even out.

- Some foods improve with reheating – casseroles in particular.

- Pastry and crunchy toppings can lose their crispness if overheated, so heat them carefully.

- Take care when heating pastry with a filling. Although the pastry may feel only warm to touch, the filling is usually much hotter.

CARE OF YOUR MICROWAVE

Look after your oven and follow the manufacturer's instructions and it will reward you with years of reliable service. Avoid operating the oven while it is empty – make sure by keeping a small container of water in the oven in case someone switches it on in error. Do not use metal containers in the oven (unless the manufacturer allows this), do not allow anything to jam in the door (tea towels, for instance) and never lean heavily on the door. Lastly, make sure that every member of the household knows how to operate the oven correctly.

Keeping a microwave oven clean is usually a simple matter of wiping out the oven after each use. The walls of the oven don't heat up during cooking, so food does not bake on them as it does in a conventional oven. This is not the case with a combination oven, however, which does heat up and, because the cavity is smaller than a conventional oven and the oven walls are closer to the cooking food, splashes can easily burn on.

Tips for cleaning microwave and combination ovens

- Wipe out the interior frequently and regularly.

- Mop up spills and splashes as soon as they occur – spilled food and splashes will only slow down the cooking the next time the oven is used.

- Removable parts, such as a turntable or a shelf, should be washed with hot water and detergent, then thoroughly dried.

- For heavy soiling, put a bowl of water in the microwave oven and cook on HIGH (100%) until it boils – the steam produced will help to soften stubborn marks, which can then be wiped away with a soft cloth.

- To remove lingering odours from the oven, add some lemon juice to the water.

- Do not use abrasive cleaners on any part of a microwave or combination oven, and never use a knife to clean off a stubborn mark.

- Never allow water or cleaning materials to enter any vents in the oven cavity.

- To clean stubborn stains from a combination oven, use liquid cleaners only.

- Look for specially-designed microwave oven cleaners too.

Replacement parts
In the event that an oven part needs replacing (such as a turntable, shelf or bulb), obtain it from an authorised service agent. To find out your nearest one, contact the manufacturer of your oven (the address and telephone number should be in your instruction book).

If a fault occurs
Always obtain qualified help – from an authorised service engineer. Never remove the outer casing of the oven or attempt to repair a fault yourself.

Servicing

If you use your oven correctly and do not move it around frequently or drop it, there's little need to have it checked. However, if you have reason to believe that the oven has been damaged in any way, or if you notice a change in its performance, you may wish to have it checked by an authorised engineer.

Many manufacturers offer a service contract on new ovens.

Leakage testing

If you look after your oven, there is little need to have it checked. A microwave oven which has been damaged sufficiently (by dropping it, for instance) to allow leakage, will not work. However, over the years many people have spoken to me, simply *wondering* whether their oven leaks. My answer is always reassuring, but I also understand that once doubts are instilled in the mind, mistrust lingers. In these instances, I suggest that it is worth putting their mind at ease by having the oven checked over by a qualified engineer.

Over recent years consumers have been tempted to buy low-cost hand-held leakage testers. They have all proved to be unreliable. At the time of publication, there is still nothing as dependable as those used by authorised engineers and environmental health officers. Their testers are substantial and costly machines which are recalibrated regularly to make sure they are accurate.

6

ABOUT THE RECIPES

- Ingredients are given in metric and imperial. Follow one type of measure for successful results.

- All spoon quantities are level unless otherwise stated.

- The recipes in this book have been tested in 750–850W microwave ovens. If your oven has a higher wattage, you can either cook on HIGH (100%) and reduce the cooking times slightly or use a lower power level which is the equivalent of 750–850W and cook for the recommended time. If your oven has less than 750W, you will need to increase the cooking times. Remember to increase or decrease by seconds.

- When a food should be covered (or uncovered) during cooking, the method states this. If no instruction is given, then it makes little difference whether you cover the food or not.

- All cooking is on HIGH (100%) unless otherwise stated.

- In ovens without turntables, food may need turning or repositioning occasionally.

- Each recipe starts with the number of servings, an approximate cooking time and a note indicating whether it is suitable for freezing.

- When a recipe benefits from using a grill, this is also indicated at the start of the recipe.

Combination ovens

There are no recipes for combination cooking (that is, using conventional oven heat together with microwaves) in this book. Instead, my colleague Caroline Young and I have created over 100 recipes for combination ovens and microwave ovens with built-in grills for *The Combination Microwave Cook*, also published in the Right Way series.

7

SOUPS AND STARTERS

Home-made soups are quick and easy in a microwave, whether you are making an individual portion or enough for a family.

Those of us who still like to make the occasional pot of good home-made stock find it convenient to put the broken-up bones, chicken carcass or well-washed vegetable peelings into a bowl, cover them with water and cook for about 20 minutes (or more, if you prefer). When the mixture is strained, you have a delicious fresh stock ready for adding to sauces and, in particular, to soups.

Tips for cooking soups
- Use a large, deep bowl so that the soup has plenty of room to boil up. This is particularly important when a recipe contains milk.

- When cooking a conventional soup recipe in the microwave, reduce the quantity of liquid by about one quarter. There is usually less evaporation in the microwave. If the finished soup is too thick, it can always be diluted after cooking.

- Cut ingredients such as vegetables into even pieces to encourage even cooking. The smaller they are cut, the quicker they will cook.

- The cooking time can be speeded up by adding *boiling* water or stock to the main ingredients (a kettle boils a large quantity of water far more efficiently than a microwave). To speed up cooking even further, use half the liquid only, then add the extra (hot) after cooking.

- Cover soup to keep the moisture and heat in. A lid with a vent helps to prevent it boiling over. If you don't have a vented lid, put a wooden cocktail stick between the bowl and lid.

- Stir the soup occasionally to encourage even cooking.

- Most soups can be cooked on HIGH (100%). Remember that the cooking time will depend on the ingredient with the longest cooking time.

- If a soup contains meat which requires tenderising, rice, pasta or other cereals, it will cook just as quickly if it is first brought to the boil on HIGH (100%), then cooked on MEDIUM (50%) or MEDIUM-LOW (30%) for the remaining time. In the same way, a soup can be left to simmer gently for as long as you wish, to develop its flavour, just as you would leave it on the hob.

- *Dried soups:* Make up the soup mix with hot water (from the kettle) following the packet instructions. Cook on HIGH

(100%), stirring occasionally, until the soup boils. Lower the microwave power to MEDIUM (50%) or MEDIUM-LOW (30%), cover and cook for the time stated on the packet, stirring occasionally.

* *Cans and cartons of soups:* Pour the soup into a bowl, diluting it according to label instructions if necessary. Cover and cook on HIGH (100%), stirring occasionally, until hot.

FRESH TOMATO SOUP   *Serves 4–6*
Cooking: 22–24 minutes on HIGH (100%)   *Will freeze*

25 g (1 oz) butter
1 bacon rasher, rind removed and finely chopped
1 medium onion, finely chopped
1 carrot, finely chopped
2 tsp sugar
450 g (1 lb) fresh tomatoes, chopped; or 400 g can chopped
    tomatoes
450 ml (¾ pint) boiling chicken stock
freshly milled salt and black pepper
bouquet garni
2 tsp lemon juice
2 tbsp tomato purée
chopped parsley to serve
croûtons or crusty bread, to serve

1. Put the butter, bacon, onion, carrot and sugar in a large bowl. Cover and cook for 4 minutes.

2. Add the remaining ingredients. Cover and cook for 18–20 minutes, stirring occasionally.

3. Allow the soup to stand for 10 minutes then remove the bouquet garni.

4. Purée the soup using a hand-held stick blender or in a food processor. (For a really smooth soup, strain through a sieve after puréeing.)

5. Reheat if necessary. Sprinkle with chopped parsley and serve with croûtons or crusty bread.

CREAM OF TOMATO SOUP
Follow method for FRESH TOMATO SOUP and stir in 150 ml (¼ pint) single or double cream, or crème fraîche before serving.

FRENCH ONION SOUP *Serves 4–6*

Cooking: soup 19–22 minutes on HIGH *(100%)*
       bread ½–1½ minutes on HIGH *(100%) or under grill*
Will freeze without the bread and cheese

40 g (1½ oz) butter
450 g (1 lb) onions, finely sliced
600 ml (1 pint) boiling beef or vegetable stock
1 tbsp Worcestershire sauce
freshly milled salt and white pepper
4 slices of French bread
75 g (2¾ oz) Cheddar or Gruyère cheese, grated

1. Put the butter and onions in a large bowl, cover and cook for 4 minutes.

2. Add the boiling stock, Worcestershire sauce and seasoning. Cover and cook for 15–18 minutes, stirring occasionally.

3. Arrange the bread slices on a plate and top with the cheese. Cook, uncovered, for ½–1½ minutes, until the cheese has melted. Float them on top of the soup, to serve.

OR

Pour the soup into a flameproof casserole dish, float the bread slices on top, sprinkle with cheese and cook under a hot grill until the cheese bubbles.

CREAM OF ONION SOUP
Follow stages 1–2 for FRENCH ONION SOUP, then purée using a hand-held stick blender or in a food processor and stir in 150 ml (¼ pint) single cream. Omit the bread and cheese. Instead, fry some onion rings in butter until crisp and brown and scatter over the soup to serve.

CREAMY BUTTER BEAN AND BACON SOUP   *Serves 4–6*
Cooking: 22 minutes on HIGH *(100%)*
Will freeze without the cream and parsley

25 g (1 oz) butter
1 medium onion, finely chopped
4 lean rashers bacon, rinds removed and finely chopped
two 410 g cans butter beans, drained
600 ml (1 pint) boiling chicken stock
¼ tsp dried mixed herbs
freshly milled salt and pepper
150 ml (¼ pint) single cream
chopped parsley, to serve

1. Put the butter, onion and bacon into a large bowl, cover and cook for 4 minutes, stirring once.

2. Add the beans, boiling stock, herbs and seasoning. Cover and cook for about 15 minutes, stirring occasionally.

3. Using a slotted spoon, lift out one or two spoonfuls of bean mixture and reserve. Purée the remaining soup using a hand-held stick blender or in a food processor and add the cream.

4. Return the soup to its bowl and add the reserved bean mixture. Reheat for 2–3 minutes if necessary, without boiling, then sprinkle with parsley to serve.

LEEK AND POTATO SOUP

Serves 4–6

Cooking: 22 minutes on HIGH *(100%)*

Will freeze

25 g (1 oz) butter
2 medium leeks, sliced
1 medium onion, finely chopped
350 g (12 oz) potatoes, finely sliced
600 ml (1 pint) boiling chicken or vegetable stock
freshly milled salt and pepper
150 ml (¼ pint) double cream
chopped chives, to serve

1. Put the butter, leeks and onion in a large bowl, cover and cook for 5 minutes, stirring once.

2. Add the potatoes, boiling stock and seasoning. Cover and cook for 15 minutes, stirring occasionally, until the vegetables are tender.

3. Purée the soup using a hand-held stick blender or in a food processor. Stir in the cream.

4. Reheat for 1–2 minutes, without boiling, and serve sprinkled with chives.

CHICKEN AND VEGETABLE SOUP   *Serves 4*
Cooking: 33–35 minutes on HIGH *(100%)*   *Will freeze*

175–225 g (6–8 oz) chicken portion
1 bay leaf
1 garlic clove
bouquet garni
1 small onion, finely chopped
1 medium carrot, diced
1 medium leek, finely sliced
1 celery stick, finely sliced
2 tbsp Worcestershire sauce
freshly milled salt and pepper

1. Put the chicken in a medium bowl with 300 ml (½ pint) water, the bay leaf, garlic and bouquet garni. Cover and cook for 20 minutes. Allow to stand for 5 minutes.

2. Meanwhile, put the onion, carrot, leek and celery into a large bowl, cover and cook for 5 minutes, stirring once or twice.

3. Lift the chicken out of its stock, discard the skin and bones and chop the chicken meat into small pieces. Strain the stock, discarding the bay leaf, garlic and bouquet garni.

4. Add the chicken to the vegetables and pour the chicken stock over. Add the Worcestershire sauce, 150 ml (¼ pint) water and seasoning to taste.

5. Cover and cook for 8–10 minutes, stirring occasionally, until the vegetables are tender.

MINTED PEA SOUP   *Serves 4*
Cooking: 10–12 minutes on HIGH (100%)   *Will freeze*

1 bunch spring onions
100 g (3½ oz) frozen peas
100 g (3½ oz) potatoes, diced
300 ml (½ pint) vegetable stock
1 tsp concentrated mint sauce
300 ml (½ pint) milk
freshly milled salt and pepper
150 ml (¼ pint) double cream

1. Chop the spring onions, reserving some of the green tops for a garnish.

2. Put the onions, peas, potatoes and stock into a large bowl. Cover and cook for 10–12 minutes, stirring once, until the vegetables are soft.

3. Allow to stand for 5 minutes, then purée the soup using a hand-held stick blender or in a food processor. Stir in the mint sauce, milk and seasoning to taste.

4. Serve immediately or allow to cool, refrigerate, and serve chilled. Top each bowl of soup with a generous swirl of cream and scatter over the reserved spring onion tops.

HADDOCK AND CORN CHOWDER   *Serves 4*

Cooking: 22 minutes on HIGH *(100%)*   *Not suitable for freezing*

450 g (1 lb) smoked haddock
300 ml (½ pint) vegetable stock
1 medium onion, finely chopped
15 g (½ oz) butter
450 g (1 lb) potatoes, diced
freshly milled salt and pepper
198 g can sweetcorn
300 ml (½ pint) milk

1. Put the haddock in a shallow dish and add the stock. Cover and cook for 5 minutes. Allow to stand for 10 minutes.

2. Meanwhile, put the onion and butter in a large bowl, cover and cook for 3 minutes.

3. Lift the haddock from its dish, reserving the stock. Skin and flake the fish, discarding any bones.

4. Add the potatoes and reserved fish stock to the onion. Cover and cook for 10 minutes, stirring once, until the potatoes are tender. Season to taste.

5. Add the haddock, the sweetcorn with its liquid and the milk. Reheat for 3–4 minutes before serving. Do not boil.

CHICKEN LIVER PÂTÉ   *Serves 4–6*
Cooking: 11 minutes on HIGH *(100%)*   *Will freeze*

25 g (1 oz) butter
1 medium onion, finely chopped
1 large garlic clove, crushed
450 g (1 lb) chicken livers
2 bay leaves
100 g (3½ oz) curd cheese
4 tbsp Greek yogurt
2 tbsp dry sherry
few drops of hot pepper sauce
parsley sprigs to garnish
crusty bread, toast or biscuits to serve

1. Put the butter, onion and garlic in a medium bowl, cover and cook for 3 minutes.

2. Stir in the livers and bay leaves. Cook uncovered for 6–8 minutes, stirring occasionally, until the livers are cooked.

3. Allow to cool. Remove and discard the bay leaves.

4. Tip the liver mixture into a blender or food processor. Add the cheese, yogurt, sherry and pepper sauce and purée until smooth. Put into a serving dish, cover and refrigerate.

5. Garnish with parsley and serve with bread, toast or biscuits.

MUSHROOMS WITH GARLIC

Cooking: about 4½ minutes on HIGH (100%)

Serves 4
Will freeze

25 g (1 oz) butter
1 garlic clove, crushed
225 g (8 oz) small button mushrooms
freshly milled salt and black pepper
1 tbsp white wine vinegar
2 tbsp chopped parsley
toast triangles to serve

1. Put the butter and garlic in a bowl and cook for 20–40 seconds until the butter has melted.

2. Stir in the mushrooms, coating them with the butter. Season lightly with salt and pepper and add the vinegar. Cover and cook for 3-4 minutes, stirring once or twice.

3. Stir in the parsley and serve with toast.

HOT COURGETTE AND TOMATO SALAD *Serves 2*
Cooking: 2–4 minutes on HIGH *(100%)*
Not suitable for freezing

1 garlic clove
25 g (1 oz) fresh breadcrumbs
2 small courgettes
2 medium tomatoes, sliced
2 tbsp French salad dressing

1. Halve the garlic clove and rub the cut sides around the inside of a small ovenproof dish. Add the breadcrumbs and cook for 1 minute, stirring frequently, until crisp and golden brown. Allow to stand.

2. Use a potato peeler to cut the courgettes into long ribbons. Arrange them on two small plates with the tomatoes. Sprinkle the dressing over them.

3. Cover and cook each plate for 1–2 minutes (or both plates for about 2–3 minutes), turning them half way through cooking.

4. Top with the crisp crumbs and serve immediately.

SMOKED HAM AND EGG RAMEKINS   *Serves 2*
Cooking: 1–1½ minutes on MEDIUM (50%)
Not suitable for freezing

1 slice lean smoked ham
2 eggs (make sure they are at room temperature)
freshly milled salt and black pepper
2 tbsp Greek yogurt
paprika

1. Halve the ham and place each piece in a ramekin dish. Break an egg into each and prick the yolks. Add a little seasoning and spoon the yogurt over.

2. Cook, uncovered, on MEDIUM (50%) for 1–1½ minutes or until the eggs are nearly set. Allow to stand for 1–2 minutes.

3. Sprinkle with paprika and serve immediately.

HOT GRAPEFRUIT WITH VERMOUTH *Serves 2*
Cooking: about 2½ minutes on HIGH (100%)
Not suitable for freezing

1 grapefruit
2–4 tsp sweet red vermouth
25 g (1 oz) butter
2 tbsp soft brown sugar
glacé cherries or orange slices to garnish

1. Halve the grapefruit and put into dishes. Use a grapefruit knife or small sharp knife to cut around and loosen each segment. Pour the vermouth over.

2. In a small bowl, melt the butter for 20 seconds and brush over the grapefruit. Sprinkle with the sugar.

3. Cook both dishes together, uncovered, for about 1–2 minutes until hot throughout.

4. Garnish with glacé cherries or orange slices and serve immediately.

TUNA AND TOMATO PASTA   *Serves 4*
Cooking: 20 minutes on HIGH (100%)
Will freeze – put the sauce and pasta in separate containers

1 medium onion, finely chopped
2 garlic cloves, crushed
400 g can chopped tomatoes
150 ml (¼ pint) dry white vermouth
1 vegetable stock cube
175 g (6 oz) pasta shapes, such as twists or shells
198 g can tuna in brine or oil, drained and flaked
2 tbsp chopped fresh herbs, such as basil, oregano or
fennel

1. Put the onion and garlic into a medium bowl, cover and cook for 2 minutes.

2. Stir in the tomatoes, vermouth and crumbled stock cube. Cover and cook for 8 minutes, stirring occasionally.

3. Put the pasta in a large bowl and cover well with boiling water. Cook, uncovered, for 7 minutes, stirring once or twice. Allow to stand for 5 minutes.

4. Meanwhile, add the tuna and herbs to the tomato sauce, cover and cook for 2–3 minutes until piping hot.

5. Drain the pasta well and serve it topped with the sauce.

SPINACH SALAD WITH HOT BACON DRESSING
Cooking: 5–6 minutes on HIGH *(100%)* *Serves 4*
Not suitable for freezing

225 g (8 oz) fresh young spinach leaves
225 g (8 oz) bacon rushers, rinds removed and chopped
2 tbsp oil
4 spring onions, finely chopped
1 tbsp white wine or cider vinegar
1 tsp soft brown sugar
1 tbsp whole grain mustard
freshly milled salt and black pepper

1. Wash, trim and dry the spinach, shredding any large leaves. Arrange them in a serving bowl.

2. Put the bacon in a medium bowl and cook, uncovered, for about 4–5 minutes, stirring occasionally, until it begins to brown and crisp. Add the remaining ingredients and cook for 1 minute.

3. Pour the bacon dressing over the spinach and serve immediately.

LEMON SOLE WITH SMOKED SALMON   *Serves 2*
Cooking: 4 minutes on HIGH (100%)
Not suitable for freezing

2 lemon sole fillets
50 g (1¾ oz) smoked salmon slices
2 tbsp dry white vermouth
3 tbsp double cream
1 tsp cornflour
2 spring onions, finely chopped
squeeze of lemon or lime juice
1 tbsp finely chopped parsley

1. Cut each sole fillet in half lengthways. Put a strip of smoked salmon on the skin side of each piece of sole. Roll each from its widest end and secure with a wooden cocktail stick.

2. Arrange the fish, spiral ends up, around the edge of a small shallow dish and add the vermouth. Cover and cook for about 2 minutes until the fish is just cooked.

3. Carefully pour the liquid from around the fish into a jug. Whisk in the cream and cornflour, then add the onions. Cook for about 2 minutes, stirring frequently, until the sauce thickens and boils. Stir in the lemon or lime juice and parsley.

4. Serve the fish with the sauce.

STUFFED MUSHROOMS *Serves 4*
Cooking: 4 minutes on HIGH *(100%)*
Not suitable for freezing

40 g (1½ oz) butter
50 g (1¾ oz) fresh breadcrumbs
50 g (1¾ oz) garlic sausage, finely chopped
50 g (1¾ oz) Cheddar cheese, finely grated
1 tbsp chopped parsley
1 tsp pesto
beaten egg
freshly milled salt and black pepper
4 large flat mushrooms
parsley sprigs to garnish

1. Put 1 tbsp of the butter in a medium bowl and cook for 20 seconds until melted. Stir in the breadcrumbs, sausage, cheese, parsley and pesto. Add sufficient beaten egg to bind the mixture. Season to taste.

2. Remove the stalks from the mushrooms, chop finely and add to the stuffing mixture. Pile the stuffing into the mushrooms and dot with the remaining butter.

3. Cover and cook for 3–4 minutes. Garnish with parsley to serve.

8

FISH

Fish is made for the microwave! It cooks quickly, keeps its shape beautifully and retains all its juices. Cook it whole or in fillets; just as it is, brushed with butter, or in a sauce. No matter which method you choose, so long as you don't overcook it, the texture and taste are wonderful.

Tips for thawing fish

- Thaw fish on DEFROST or MEDIUM-LOW (30%).

- Cover it to ensure even thawing.

- Separate pieces and reposition them as they begin to thaw.

- Take care not to overheat or the fish will start to cook around the edges. If any areas start to feel warm, stop thawing and allow the fish to stand for 5–10 minutes before continuing.

Guide to thawing times	
	on DEFROST or MEDIUM-LOW (30%):
Whole round fish	4–6 minutes per 450 g (1 lb)
Whole flat fish	3–4 minutes per 450 g (1 lb)
Cutlets, steaks and fillets	3–4 minutes per 450 g (1 lb)
Prawns and shrimps	2–3 minutes per 100 g (3¼ oz)
	3–4 minutes per 225 g (8 oz)
Scallops	3–4 minutes per 225 g (8 oz)

Tips for cooking fish
- Make a few slits in the skin of whole fish. This allows steam to escape and prevents the skin from bursting open.

- Use a shallow dish, unless you are cooking fish in a sauce, casserole or soup.

- Arrange fish in an even layer to encourage it to cook evenly. When cooking whole fish, overlap their tails, or lay them side by side with head to tail. With fillets, either roll them up and secure each with a wooden cocktail stick, or tuck the thin ends underneath the thick ends to achieve an even layer. When cooking fish steaks, arrange them with the thinner ends towards the centre of the dish.

- Season with salt after cooking to prevent the fish drying out and the surface from toughening.

- When cooking with butter, best results are achieved if it is melted first and brushed over the fish.

- Cover during cooking, to keep the moisture in.

- Turn the whole fish once during cooking.

- Take care not to overcook fish. Shellfish cooks especially quickly and is easily overcooked – for this reason add it to a dish towards the end of cooking.

- Should you find that fish easily overcooks on HIGH (100%), try using a lower power level and cooking for slightly longer.

- Check that fish is cooked by lifting up the flakes with a fork. If it is still slightly undercooked, just lay the flakes back down again and allow the fish to stand and the temperature to even out – the flakes should turn opaque and cook to perfection.

- Allow cooked fish to stand for 3–5 minutes before serving.

- *Boil-in-the-bag* fish can be cooked in its bag. Remember to pierce the bag before cooking.

- *Fish in breadcrumbs or batter is* generally not suitable for microwave cooking, though fish fingers are acceptable when cooked on a browning dish (follow the dish manufacturer's instructions).

Guide to cooking times	
	per 450 g (1 lb) on HIGH (100%):
Whole round fish	4 minutes
Whole flat fish	3 minutes
Steak, cutlets and thick fillets	4–6 minutes
Thin fillets	2–3 minutes
Prawns, raw	2–4 minutes
Scallops, shelled	2–3 minutes, adding corals for final 1–2 minutes

If you find that fish cooked on HIGH (100%) tends to spit and overcook, try reducing the power to MEDIUM (50%) and cooking for a little longer.

FISH – Basic method

1. Put the fish in an even layer in a shallow dish. If wished, brush with melted butter, or add 2 tbsp water, stock, milk or wine.

2. Cover and cook, using the times above as a guide.

3. Allow to stand for 3–5 minutes before serving.

MUSSELS – Basic method

1. Put 450–900 g (1–2 lb) cleaned and unopened mussels in a
   large bowl. Add 150 ml (¼ pint) stock, wine or water and a
   little finely chopped onion and garlic.

2. Cover and cook for 3–5 minutes, shaking the bowl
   occasionally and removing mussels from the top as they
   cook. Discard any that refuse to open. Use a slotted spoon
   to lift the mussels on to a warm dish.

3. Season the sauce with salt and pepper, add some chopped
   fresh herbs and, if wished, stir in 3 tbsp double cream
   before pouring over the mussels and serving.

PLAICE WITH LEMON SAUCE   *Serves 2*

Cooking: about 7 minutes on HIGH (100%)
Not suitable for freezing

1 tbsp butter
4 plaice fillets, skinned
2 tbsp chopped parsley
2 tsp cornflour
grated rind and juice of half a lemon
3 tbsp white wine
½ tsp sugar
freshly milled salt and pepper

1. Heat the butter for 20 seconds until melted. Brush over the skinned side of each plaice fillet. Sprinkle the parsley over. Roll up the fillets from the thick end and arrange them in a shallow dish.

2. Cover and cook for 3–4 minutes. Allow to stand for 3 minutes.

3. Meanwhile, put the cornflour into a bowl or jug and whisk in the remaining ingredients.

4. Cook, uncovered for 1–2 minutes, stirring occasionally, until the sauce thickens and boils.

5. Pour the sauce over the fish and reheat for 30 seconds. Serve immediately.

PLAICE WITH ORANGE SAUCE

Follow the method for PLAICE WITH LEMON SAUCE, using orange rind and juice instead of lemon rind and juice.

TROUT WITH ALMONDS   *Serves 2*
Cooking: 6 minutes on HIGH *(100%)*
Not suitable for freezing

**2 trout, each weighing about 225 g (8 oz), cleaned and
    heads removed**
freshly milled salt and pepper
25 g (1 oz) butter
25 g (1 oz) flaked almonds
lemon wedges to serve

1. Using a sharp knife, make one or two shallow slits in the
   skin on each side of the trout. Season inside with salt and
   pepper.

2. Heat half the butter for 20 seconds until melted. Brush the
   trout with butter, then arrange them, head to tail, in a
   shallow dish.

3. Cover and cook for about 3–4 minutes or until just cooked,
   gently turning the fish over half way through cooking.
   Keep warm.

4. Meanwhile, put the remaining butter in a heatproof dish
   and heat for 10 seconds until melted. Stir in the almonds
   and cook for 1–2 minutes, stirring frequently, until golden
   brown.

5. Pour the almonds and butter over the trout and serve
   immediately with lemon wedges.

FISH IN PAPER PARCELS   *Serves 4*

Cooking: 7–9 minutes on HIGH (100%)
Not suitable for freezing

4 baby carrots, cut into thin matchsticks
4 spring onions, finely sliced
50 g (1¾ oz) mushrooms, finely sliced
oil
4 fish steaks, such as cod, salmon or halibut, each
**   weighing about 175 g (6 oz)**
2 tbsp chopped fresh herbs, such as dill, fennel or parsley
50 g (1¾ oz) butter

1. Put the carrots, onions and mushrooms in a small bowl, cover and cook for 3–4 minutes.

2. Meanwhile, cut four rectangles of greaseproof paper, each large enough to wrap one piece of fish generously. Brush each sheet with a little oil.

3. Put a fish portion in the centre of each sheet of paper and top with the vegetables. Sprinkle over any liquid from the vegetables.

4. Blend the herbs into the butter and top each pile of vegetables with the seasoned butter.

5. Fold the paper over the fish and tuck the short ends underneath to form neat parcels. Arrange in a shallow dish.

6. Cook for about 4–5 minutes or until the fish is just cooked. Allow to stand for 2–3 minutes. Serve the fish in the paper so each person can enjoy the delicious aroma as the individual parcels are opened.

FISH WITH SUMMER DRESSING   *Serves 4*
Cooking: 6–7 minutes on HIGH *(100%)*
Not suitable for freezing

**4 fillets of white fish, such as cod or haddock, each
   weighing about 175 g (6 oz)
2 tsp lemon juice or white wine vinegar
150 g (5½ oz) Greek yogurt
½ tsp concentrated mint sauce
10 cm (4 inch) piece of cucumber, skinned, seeds
   removed and diced
50 g (1¼ oz) seedless green grapes, halved
freshly milled salt and pepper
thin cucumber slices to garnish**

1. Arrange the fish fillets in a shallow dish and sprinkle with
   the lemon juice or vinegar. Cover and cook for 3–4
   minutes.

2. Mix together the yogurt, mint sauce and cucumber.
   Reserve some grapes for garnish, then stir the remainder
   into the yogurt mixture. Season lightly with salt and
   pepper. Spread evenly over the fish.

3. Cook for a further 3 minutes or until the fish is just cooked.
   Allow to stand for 2–3 minutes. Serve garnished with
   cucumber slices and the reserved grapes.

SALMON WITH CREAMY CHIVE SAUCE *Serves 2*
Cooking: 7½–8½ minutes on HIGH (100%)
Not suitable for freezing

2 salmon cutlets or fillets
150 ml (¼ pint) vegetable stock
100 ml (3½ fl oz) dry white vermouth
1 tbsp lemon juice
2 tbsp chopped chives
5 tbsp double cream
freshly milled salt and pepper

1. Put the salmon in a shallow dish and add the stock and vermouth. Cover and cook for 3–4 minutes or until the fish is just cooked.

2. Lift the salmon on to a serving plate and keep warm.

3. Cook the remaining liquid, uncovered, for 4 minutes or until reduced by half. Stir in the lemon juice, chives and cream. Season to taste with salt and pepper, then cook for 30 seconds. Serve the sauce with the salmon.

PRANS À LA PROVENÇALE   *Serves 4*

Cooking: 12–15 minutes on HIGH *(100%)*
Not suitable for freezing

2 tsp olive oil
1 medium onion, finely chopped
1 garlic clove, crushed
1 green pepper, seeds removed and finely chopped
1 celery stick, finely sliced
2 tbsp cornflour
400 g can chopped tomatoes
½ tsp sugar
freshly milled salt and black pepper
1 tbsp chopped dill
350 g (12 oz) cooked shelled prawns, thawed if frozen
cooked rice or pasta to serve

1. Put the oil, onion, garlic, pepper and celery in a bowl, cover and cook for 4 minutes, stirring once or twice.

2. Stir in the cornflour, then add the tomatoes, sugar and a little seasoning. Cover and cook for 6–8 minutes, stirring once or twice.

3. Add the prawns and dill, stir, then cook for 2–3 minutes. Allow to stand for 2–3 minutes before serving with rice or pasta.

MARINATED PRAWN KEBABS *Serves 4*

Cooking: 4 minutes on HIGH (100%) plus marinating
Not suitable for freezing

16 large raw prawns, heads removed
3 tbsp clear honey
1 tbsp lemon juice or white wine vinegar
2 tbsp light soy sauce
2 tbsp tomato ketchup
green salad and lemon wedges to serve

1. Thread the prawns onto four bamboo skewers, leaving a small gap between each prawn. Lay them in a shallow dish.

2. Mix together the remaining ingredients and pour over the prawns, coating them well. Cover and marinate for about two hours, turning the skewers occasionally.

3. Lift the skewers out of the marinade and arrange them on a plate – either around the edge, or like the spokes of a wheel.

4. Cook, uncovered, for 3–4 minutes, rearranging them half way through, or until the prawns are cooked (they will turn pink).

5. Serve with green salad and lemon wedges.

FISH AND BUTTER BEAN CASSEROLE   *Serves 4*

Cooking: 14–16 minutes on HIGH (100%)
Not suitable for freezing

25 g (1 oz) butter
1 bunch spring onions, chopped
2 tbsp flour
150 ml (¼ pint) vegetable or fish stock
300 ml (½ pint) milk
4 tbsp dry white wine
2 tbsp chopped fresh parsley
450 g (1 lb) white fish, such as cod, haddock, whiting or
   plaice, skinned and boned
450 g (1 lb) smoked fish, such as haddock or cod, skinned
   and boned
415 g can butter beans, drained
freshly milled salt and pepper

1. Put the butter and onions in a large casserole dish, cover
   and cook for 2 minutes.

2. Stir in the flour, then gradually stir in the stock and milk.
   Cook for 4 minutes, stirring frequently, until boiling.

3. Add the wine and parsley. Cut the fish into chunks and add
   to the casserole. Stir in the butter beans and season to taste.

4. Cover and cook for 8–10 minutes, stirring gently once or
   twice, until the fish is cooked. Serve immediately.

LEMON SOLE WITH SMOKED SALMON – see page 54.

HADDOCK AND CORN CHOWDER – see page 46.

TUNA AND TOMATO PASTA – see page 52.

9

SAUCES

Sauces are quick and easy to make in the microwave because they can be cooked in a serving jug or bowl. Even small quantities cook well without sticking or burning, as they often do in a saucepan on the hob. Most sauces reheat well in the microwave too.

Tips for cooking sauces

- Use a jug or bowl which is large enough to allow the sauce to boil up.

- Don't bother to cover the container – you need to stir the sauce often and a cover can be a nuisance.

- Most sauces can be cooked on HIGH (100%), but those containing eggs are best cooked on MEDIUM (50%) or MEDIUM-LOW (30%) to prevent them curdling.

- Stir or whisk sauces frequently during cooking to prevent lumps forming.

- To develop the flavour of a cooked sauce (such as tomato sauce), or to thicken or reduce it further, continue cooking, uncovered, on MEDIUM (50%) or MEDIUM-LOW

(30%) until the desired flavour and consistency are achieved.

Reheat sauces on HIGH (100%), stirring occasionally.

Frozen sauces can be reheated straight from the freezer. Put the frozen block in a bowl and cook on HIGH (100%), breaking up the sauce as it thaws. Once it has thawed, stir or whisk the sauce occasionally during reheating.

WHITE SAUCE   *Serves 4*
Cooking: 3–5 minutes on HIGH *(100%)*   *Will freeze*

Serve with vegetables, fish or ham.

40 g (1½ oz) butter
40 g (1½ oz) flour
600 ml (1 pint) milk
freshly milled salt and pepper

1. Put the butter in a bowl or jug. Cook for 30 seconds until melted.

2. Stir in the flour, then gradually blend in the milk. Season to taste.

3. Cook, uncovered, for 3–5 minutes, whisking frequently.

CHEESE SAUCE
Follow the method for WHITE SAUCE and add 75–100 g (2¾–3½ oz) grated cheese to the cooked sauce. Stir until melted.

MUSHROOM SAUCE
Follow the method for WHITE SAUCE. At stage 1, add 100 g (3½ oz) finely sliced or chopped mushrooms to the butter, cover and cook for 1–2 minutes.

MUSTARD SAUCE
Follow the method for WHITE SAUCE. Add 2 tbsp ready-made mustard to the cooked sauce.

ONION SAUCE
Follow the method for WHITE SAUCE. At stage 1, add a finely chopped onion to the butter, cover and cook for 2–3 minutes.

PARSLEY SAUCE
Follow the method for WHITE SAUCE and add 2–3 tbsp chopped parsley to the cooked sauce.

PRAWN SAUCE
Follow the method for WHITE SAUCE. Add 100 g (3½ oz) small peeled prawns and 1 tbsp lemon juice to the cooked sauce. Cook for 40–60 seconds.

BREAD SAUCE   *Serves 4–6*
Cooking: 3–5 minutes on HIGH (100%),   *Will freeze*
10 minutes on MEDIUM-LOW (30%) and
3–5 minutes on MEDIUM (50%)

Serve with turkey or chicken.

1 small onion, finely sliced
1 bayleaf
6 black peppercorns
2 cloves
pinch of ground nutmeg
300 ml (½ pint) milk
50 g (1¾ oz) fresh white breadcrumbs
freshly milled salt and pepper
25 g (1 oz) butter

1. Put the onion, bay leaf, peppercorns, cloves, nutmeg and
   milk into a large bowl or jug. Cook, uncovered, on HIGH
   (100%) for 3–5 minutes or until just boiling.

2. Cover and continue cooking on MEDIUM-LOW (30%) for 10
   minutes.

3. Strain and return the milk to the bowl or jug. Stir in the
   breadcrumbs, season to taste and add butter.

4. Cover and cook on MEDIUM (50%) for 3–5 minutes, stirring
   occasionally.

CREAMY CURRY SAUCE   *Serves 4–6*
Cooking: 5–6 minutes on HIGH (100%) and   *Will freeze*
8–10 minutes on MEDIUM (50%)

Serve with hard-boiled eggs, vegetables, fish, meat or poultry.

1 tbsp oil
1 large onion, finely chopped
1 garlic clove, crushed
1 large eating apple, peeled, cored and chopped
1 tbsp flour
300 ml (½ pint) vegetable or chicken stock
2 tbsp curry paste
1 tbsp tomato purée
2 tbsp coconut cream
1 tbsp lemon juice
freshly milled salt and pepper
150 ml (¼ pint) single cream

1. Put the oil, onion and garlic into a bowl or jug, cover and
   cook for 3 minutes.

2. Add the apple and then stir in the flour. Blend in the stock,
   curry paste, tomato purée and coconut cream.

3. Cook for 2–3 minutes or until the sauce boils, then cook on
   MEDIUM (50%) for 8–10 minutes, stirring occasionally.

4. Stir in the lemon juice and season with salt and pepper.
   Add the cream and cook for 40 seconds.

BOLOGNESE SAUCE *Serves 4*
Cooking: 24–29 minutes on HIGH *(100%)* *Will freeze*

Serve with pasta, noodles, or as filling for jacket potatoes
(page 130).

1 tbsp oil
1 large onion, finely chopped
1 garlic clove, crushed
100 g (3½ oz) streaky bacon, finely chopped
2 medium carrots, finely chopped
450 g (1 lb) lean minced beef
150 ml (¼ pint) beef stock
2 tbsp tomato purée
½ tsp dried mixed herbs
½ tsp dried oregano
freshly milled salt and pepper

1. Put the oil, onion, garlic, bacon and carrots in a large bowl.
   Cover and cook for 4 minutes, stirring once.

2. Break up the minced beef and add to the bowl. Cover and
   cook for 5 minutes, stirring once.

3. Add the remaining ingredients and stir well. Cover and
   cook for 15–20 minutes, stirring occasionally.

BARBECUE SAUCE   *Serves 4*
Cooking: 10–12 minutes on HIGH (100%)   *Will freeze*

Serve with burgers, steaks, poultry or vegetables.

1 tbsp oil
1 large onion, finely chopped
300 ml (½ pint) vegetable stock
3 tbsp red wine vinegar
3 tbsp brown sugar
3 tbsp tomato purée
3 tbsp Worcestershire sauce
1 tbsp ready-made mustard
1 tbsp chopped mixed herbs such as parsley, oregano,
**   marjoram**
freshly milled salt and pepper

1. Put the oil and onion in a bowl, cover and cook for 4
   minutes, stirring once.

2. Stir in the remaining ingredients, cover and cook for 6–8
   minutes, stirring once or twice. For a thicker sauce,
   uncover and continue cooking, stirring occasionally, until
   the required consistency is achieved.

APPLE SAUCE   *Serves 4*
Cooking: 5 minutes on HIGH *(100%)*   *Will freeze*

Serve with roast pork, duck or goose.

225 g (8 oz) cooking apples, peeled, cored and sliced
2 tsp caster sugar (optional)
small knob of butter

1. Put the apples in a bowl with 1 tbsp water and the sugar (optional).

2. Cover and cook for 5 minutes, stirring occasionally, or until the apples are soft and partially puréed.

3. Stir in the butter and serve hot or cold.

TOMATO SAUCE   *Serves 4–6*
Cooking: 8–11 minutes on HIGH *(100%)*   *Will freeze*

Serve with pasta, noodles, vegetables, fish, meat or poultry.

2 tsp oil
1 small onion, finely chopped
1 small carrot, finely chopped
1 garlic clove, crushed
1 tbsp cornflour
400 g can chopped tomatoes or 450 g (1 lb) fresh ripe
  tomatoes, skinned and chopped
300 ml (½ pint) chicken or vegetable stock
1 tbsp sugar
1 tbsp tomato purée
freshly milled salt and black pepper

1. Put the oil, onion, carrot and garlic in a bowl or jug, cover
   and cook for 2–3 minutes.

2. Stir in the cornflour, then add the remaining ingredients.

3. Cover and cook for 6–8 minutes, stirring occasionally.

JAM SAUCE   *Serves 4*
Cooking: 2½ minutes on HIGH *(100%)*   *Will freeze*

Serve hot with sponge puddings; pancakes, or, hot or cold,
with ice cream.

4 tbsp jam or conserve
2 tsp cornflour

1. Put the jam in a bowl or jug and add 150 ml (¼ pint) boiling
   water. Cook for 1 minute and stir well until the jam melts.

2. Mix the cornflour to a smooth paste with a little water. Stir
   into the jam mixture.

3. Cook for 1–1½ minutes, stirring frequently, until the sauce
   thickens and boils.

HOLLANDAISE SAUCE
Serves 4
Cooking: 1½–2 minutes on HIGH (100%)
Not suitable for freezing

Serve with fish (salmon is a favourite) or vegetables (asparagus is traditional).

100 g (3½ oz) butter
2 tbsp white wine vinegar
2 large egg yolks
freshly milled salt and pepper

1. Cut the butter into small pieces and put into a bowl. Cook for 30 seconds until just melted (stir to help it melt if necessary – the butter must not get too hot).

2. Add the vinegar, egg yolks and a little seasoning. Whisk well.

3. Cook, whisking after every 10 seconds, until the sauce thickens. Take care not to over-cook or the sauce will curdle.

CHOCOLATE SAUCE *Serves 4–6*
Cooking: 3 minutes on MEDIUM *(50%)* *Will freeze*

Serve with ice cream, chocolate sponge pudding, pancakes,
waffles, bananas or poached pears.

175 g (6 oz) plain chocolate
3 tbsp golden syrup
25 g (1 oz) butter
1 tbsp lemon juice

1. Break the chocolate into a bowl. Add the remaining ingredients plus 2 tbsp water.

2. Cook, uncovered, on MEDIUM (50%) for 3 minutes, stirring occasionally, until melted, smooth and glossy.

SWEET WHITE SAUCE   *Serves 4*
Cooking: 2–4 minutes on HIGH *(100%)*   *Will freeze*

Serve with sponge and fruit puddings.

15 g (½ oz) cornflour
300 ml (½ pint) milk
knob of butter
1 tbsp caster sugar
few drops of vanilla extract

1. In a bowl or jug, mix the cornflour to a smooth paste with
   a little of the milk.

2. Heat the remaining milk for 1–2 minutes. Pour on to the
   cornflour mixture and whisk well.

3. Cook for 1–2 minutes, whisking frequently, until the sauce
   thickens and boils.

4. Stir in the butter, sugar and vanilla extract.

BRANDY SAUCE
Follow method for SWEET WINE SAUCE. At stage 4, add 2 tbsp
brandy.

SUMMER FRUIT SAUCE *Serves 6*
Cooking: 7 minutes on HIGH (100%) *Will freeze*

Serve with ice cream, pancakes, meringues, poached fruit or
sponge puddings.

225 g (8 oz) frozen summer fruit
175 g (6 oz) redcurrant jelly
2 tbsp port
2 tsp cornflour

1. Put the fruit in a bowl and cook for 3 minutes, stirring
   once, until thawed.

2. Add the jelly and port. Cook for 3 minutes, stirring
   frequently, or until the jelly has melted.

3. Mix the cornflour to a smooth paste with a little water. Add
   a little of the warm fruit, then stir the mixture into the bowl.

4. Cook for 1 minute or until the sauce thickens and boils.

BUTTERSCOTCH SAUCE   *Serves 4*
Cooking: 3½ minutes on HIGH *(100%)*   *Will freeze*

Serve with ice cream or sponge puddings.

50 g (1¾ oz) butter
50 g (1¾ oz) brown sugar
175 g (6 oz) golden syrup
2 tsp lemon juice
150 ml (¼ pint) double cream

1. Put the butter, sugar and syrup into a bowl or jug and cook for 2–3 minutes until melted.

2. Stir until well blended.

3. Stir in the lemon juice and cream. Heat for 30 seconds before serving.

10

MEAT AND POULTRY

Meat and poultry can be thawed and cooked in the microwave oven. It is particularly suitable for bacon rashers and joints; whole poultry and poultry pieces; minced meat; and cubes of beef, pork, lamb, bacon and poultry for cooking in a sauce.

The results with joints of meat, chops and steaks depend on personal taste, unless you have a combination oven (which browns and crisps as well as cooking quickly with microwaves). Here, you will find plenty of tips on how to get the best results.

Tips for thawing meat and poultry
• Remove any metal tags from the wrappings.

- Stand the meat or poultry on a microwave or roasting rack – to lift it above the liquid which collects beneath.

- Thaw on DEFROST or MEDIUM-LOW (30%).

- Thawing times are only a guide as all microwave ovens vary and all meat and poultry are different shapes and sizes.

- Separate items like bacon rashers, chops and steaks as they begin to thaw. Reposition them occasionally too.

- Turn large pieces, joints and whole birds over at least once during thawing.

Guide to thawing times	
Per 450 g (1 lb) on DEFROST or MEDIUM-LOW (30%):	
Beef joints, on bone 　　　　　　　boneless Beef, steak	10–12 minutes 8–10 minutes 8–10 minutes
Lamb joints	5–6 minutes
Pork/bacon joints	7–8 minutes
Chops	8–10 minutes
Cubed & minced meat	7–10 minutes
Liver & kidney	7–9 minutes
Chicken, whole	6–8 minutes
Turkey, whole	10–12 minutes
Chicken & turkey portions	5–7 minutes

- Pour away any moisture as it collects around the meat or poultry during thawing. If you don't, the liquid will heat up while the rest remains frozen.

- If any areas begin to warm up, stop thawing and allow a standing period of about 20 minutes before continuing.

- When thawing is completed, allow small pieces to stand for at least 10 minutes before cooking. Large pieces, whole poultry and joints need at least 30 minutes.

Tips for cooking meat and poultry
- Thaw meat and poultry completely before cooking.

- Regular shapes, such as boned and rolled joints, cook more evenly than irregular shapes, such as a leg joint.

- Meat on the bone cooks more quickly than off the bone.

- Secure large items with string or with wooden (not metal) skewers.

- Season with salt after cooking, to prevent the sauce from drying and shrinking. If the meat or poultry is immersed in liquid, a little salt can be added prior to cooking.

- Put large pieces and joints on a microwave or roasting rack, so they do not sit in their juices during cooking.

- A browning dish is useful for cooking chops and sausages (follow the dish manufacturer's instructions).

- Arrange small pieces, like chops or chicken drumsticks, with their thinner ends towards the centre of the dish.

- Arrange small even-shaped pieces, such as meatballs, around the edge of the dish.

- Meat loaves cook best in a ring-shaped mould.

- Cover during cooking to keep moisture in, to help the meat or poultry to cook evenly, and to keep the oven walls free from splashes.

- Cover joints or whole poultry with a split roasting bag, to encourage a little browning of the surface.

- Joints and whole poultry are usually cooked on HIGH (100%) (see ** in cooking guide opposite). Meat and poultry which is immersed in liquid can be brought to the boil on HIGH (100%), then cooked on MEDIUM (50%) or MEDIUM-LOW (30%) until the meat or poultry is tender – just like boiling and simmering on the hob.

- Turn large pieces, whole poultry and joints at least once during cooking.

- Stir casserole-style dishes occasionally during cooking.

- Check that meat and poultry is cooked by inserting a skewer into the thickest part. The juices should always run clear from pork and poultry, though you may prefer them pink in beef and lamb. If you use a meat thermometer, insert it into the thickest part of the meat and make sure it does not touch any bone.

- Allow joints and whole poultry to stand for 15–20 minutes after cooking – to allow the temperature to even out and to make carving easier.

Guide to cooking times	
	Per 450 g (1 lb) on HIGH *(100%):*
Beef, rare 　　　medium 　　　well done	5–6 minutes 6–7 minutes 8–9 minutes
Lamb, medium 　　　well done	7–8 minutes 8–10 minutes
Pork	8–10 minutes
Bacon	9–12 minutes
Liver and kidney	6–8 minutes
Chicken, whole	8–10 minutes
Turkey, whole	9–11 minutes
Chicken and turkey portions	6–8 minutes

** *If you find that meat and poultry cooked on* HIGH *(100%) overcooks, try cooking on* HIGH *(100%) for the first few minutes, then reducing the power to* MEDIUM-HIGH *(75%) or* MEDIUM *(50%) until cooked through.*

	on HIGH *(100%):*
Chops, 1 　　　　2 　　　　3 　　　　4	2–4 minutes 3–5 minutes 4–6 minutes 5–7 minutes
Bacon rashers, 2 　　　　　　4 　　　　　　6	2–3 minutes 4–5 minutes 5–6 minutes
Chicken breast, boneless	2–3 minutes

BEEF IN STOUT

Serves 4

Cooking: 11 minutes on HIGH (100%) and
1–1¼ hours on MEDIUM-LOW (30%)

Will freeze

2 rashers streaky bacon, chopped
225 g (8 oz) leeks, thinly sliced
2 celery sticks, thinly sliced
25 g (1 oz) flour
freshly milled salt and pepper
700 g (1 lb 9 oz) lean braising beef, cubed
2 beef stock cubes
300 ml (½ pint) stout
175 g (6 oz) ready-to-eat dried prunes
2 tbsp tomato purée
1 tsp dried mixed herbs

1. Put the bacon, leeks and celery in a large casserole, cover and cook for 3 minutes, stirring once.

2. Meanwhile, season the flour with salt and pepper and toss the beef in it until well coated. Stir the beef and any excess flour into the vegetables.

3. Dissolve the stock cubes in 4 tbsp boiling water and add to the casserole with the remaining ingredients. Stir well.

4. Cover and cook for 6–8 minutes or until boiling. Continue cooking on MEDIUM-LOW (30%) for 1–1¼ hours, stirring occasionally, until the beef is tender.

BEEF AND VEGETABLE CASSEROLE *Serves 4*
Cooking: 12 minutes on HIGH (100%) and *Will freeze*
1–1¼ hours on MEDIUM-LOW (30%)

2 tsp oil
1 medium onion, sliced
2 celery sticks, sliced
225 g (8 oz) carrots, sliced
225 g (8 oz) parsnip, swede or turnip, chopped
450 g (1 lb) lean braising beef, cubed
2 tbsp flour
300 ml (½ pint) beef stock
1 tbsp mixed dried herbs
2 tsp mustard powder
2 tbsp tomato purée
freshly milled salt and pepper

1. Put the oil and vegetables into a large casserole dish, cover and cook for 3 minutes, stirring once.

2. Add the beef, cover and cook for 4–5 minutes, stirring once.

3. Stir in the flour, then add the remaining ingredients.

4. Cover and cook for 4 minutes, then continue cooking, covered, on MEDIUM-LOW (30%) for 1–1¼ hours, stirring occasionally, until the beef is tender.

BEEF WITH GINGER AND SPRING ONIONS   *Serves 2*
Cooking: 6 minutes on HIGH *(100%) plus marinating*
Not suitable for freezing

350 g (12 oz) fillet steak
1 tbsp finely grated fresh root ginger
1 garlic clove, crushed
4 tbsp dry sherry
4 tbsp light soy sauce
1 tsp clear honey
2 tsp oil
4 tsp cornflour
1 bunch spring onions, thickly sliced
cooked rice to serve

1. Cut the steak into thin strips across the grain and put into a bowl. Mix together the ginger, garlic, sherry, soy sauce and honey. Pour the mixture over the steak, stirring to coat it well. Cover and marinate in a cool place for 1 hour or more.

2. Put the oil into a large bowl. Use a slotted spoon to lift the steak out of its marinade and stir the steak into the oil. Cook, uncovered for 2 minutes, or until the steak is just cooked, stirring once.

3. Whisk the cornflour into the marinade and pour over the steak.

4. Add the onions and cook, uncovered, for 3–4 minutes, stirring frequently, until the sauce thickens and boils. Serve with rice.

ALL SEASONS BEEF PIE *Serves 4*
Cooking: 13 minutes on HIGH *(100%) and* *Will freeze*
20–25 minutes on MEDIUM *(50%) plus grilling*

2 tsp oil
2 medium onions, finely chopped
450 g (1 lb) lean minced beef
1 beef stock cube
195 g can sweetcorn with peppers
1 tbsp dried mixed herbs
2 tbsp tomato purée
2 tsp flour
freshly milled salt and pepper
450 g (1 lb) potatoes, thinly sliced
25 g (1 oz) butter

1. Put the oil and onions in a large bowl, cover and cook for 3 minutes, stirring once.

2. Break up the beef and stir into the onions. Add the crumbled stock cube, sweetcorn with peppers, herbs, tomato purée, flour and seasoning. Stir well.

3. Cover and cook for 8–10 minutes, stirring twice.

4. Empty the beef mixture into a flameproof dish. Arrange the potatoes on top, seasoning the layers lightly with salt and pepper.

5. Put the butter in a small bowl, cook for 20 seconds or until melted and brush it over the top of the potatoes. Cover and cook on MEDIUM (50%) for 20–25 minutes until the potatoes are cooked through (test with a skewer or knife).

6. Before serving, put under a hot grill to brown and crisp the top.

MEATBALLS IN SPICY SAUCE

Serves 4

Cooking: 6 minutes on HIGH *(100%) and*   *Will freeze*
10–12 minutes on MEDIUM *(50%)*

450 g (1 lb) lean minced beef
1 small onion, finely chopped
1 tbsp dried mixed herbs
1 medium egg, beaten
150 ml (¼ pint) beef stock
1 tbsp horseradish sauce
1 tbsp Worcestershire sauce
1 tbsp tomato purée
2 tsp cornflour
few drops of hot chilli sauce
freshly milled salt and pepper

1. Mix together the beef, onion, herbs and egg and shape into 16 balls. Arrange them in a large shallow dish and cook, uncovered for 6 minutes, rearranging them half way through cooking.

2. Whisk together the remaining ingredients and pour over and around the meatballs. Cover and cook on MEDIUM (50%) for 10–12 minutes, stirring gently occasionally.

LAMB WITH SPICED MINT SAUCE   *Serves 4*
Cooking: 11 minutes on HIGH *(100%) and*   *Will freeze*
18–20 minutes on MEDIUM *(50%)*

1 medium onion, thinly sliced
½ tsp ground coriander
½ tsp ground cumin
450 g (1 lb) fillet or leg of lamb, thinly sliced
350 g (12 oz) button mushrooms
1 tbsp flour
150 ml (¼ pint) lamb or chicken stock
2 tbsp white wine vinegar
3 tbsp mint jelly
natural yogurt, to serve

1. Put the onion in a large bowl, cover and cook for 2 minutes.

2. Meanwhile, sprinkle the spices over the lamb and toss to coat the slices well.

3. Add the lamb to the onion and stir in the mushrooms. Cover and cook for 4 minutes, stirring once or twice.

4. Stir in the flour, then gradually add the stock. Add the vinegar and the mint jelly.

5. Cook for 4–5 minutes, stirring once or twice, or until boiling. Cover and continue cooking on MEDIUM (50%) for 18–20 minutes, stirring occasionally, until the lamb is tender.

6. Serve, topped with a spoonful or two of yogurt.

LAMB CURRY   *Serves 4*
Cooking: 10 minutes on HIGH *(100%) and*   *Will freeze*
18–22 minutes on MEDIUM *(50%)*

1 medium onion, sliced
2 garlic cloves, crushed
2 tbsp curry powder
700 g (1 lb 9 oz) fillet or leg of lamb, cubed
400 g can chopped tomatoes
1 lamb or beef stock cube
freshly milled salt and pepper
cooked rice, poppadoms (see opposite) and mango
    chutney, to serve

1. Put the onion and garlic in a large bowl, cover and cook for
   2–3 minutes.

2. Meanwhile, sprinkle the curry powder over the lamb and
   toss to coat the cubes well.

3. Stir the lamb into the onion. Add the tomatoes and crumble
   in the stock cube.

4. Cover and cook for 6–7 minutes or until boiling, stirring
   once or twice. Continue cooking on MEDIUM (50%)
   for about 18–22 minutes, stirring occasionally, until
   the lamb is tender. Half way through cooking, season to
   taste and remove the lid so that the sauce reduces and
   thickens.

POPPADOMS

With oil:

Brush one poppadom on one side with a little oil and place it on a sheet of paper towel. Cook for 40–60 seconds until crisp and puffed up.

Without oil:

Put two poppadoms on a sheet of paper towel and cook for 1–1¼ minutes until crisp and puffed up.

MEDITERRANEAN LAMB   *Serves 4*
Cooking: 11 minutes on HIGH *(100%) and*   *Will freeze*
20 minutes on MEDIUM *(50%)*

2 tsp olive oil
1 medium onion, thinly sliced
1 tbsp sugar
1 large aubergine, cubed
100 g (3½ oz) button mushrooms, thickly sliced
1 red pepper, seeded and sliced
450 g (1 lb) fillet or leg of lamb, thinly sliced
150 ml (¼ pint) lamb stock
150 ml (¼ pint) red wine
2 tbsp tomato purée
1 tbsp chopped oregano leaves
freshly milled salt and pepper
cooked rice or pasta, to serve

1. Put the oil, onion and sugar in a large bowl, cover and cook
   for 2 minutes.

2. Add the aubergine, mushrooms and pepper. Cover and
   cook for 2–3 minutes.

3. Stir in the lamb, then add the stock, wine, tomato purée,
   oregano and seasoning.

4. Cover and cook for 6 minutes, stirring once or twice, or
   until boiling. Continue cooking, covered, on MEDIUM
   (50%) for 20 minutes, stirring occasionally, until the lamb
   is tender.

5. Serve with rice or pasta.

LAMB KORMA *Serves 4*
Cooking: 7 minutes on HIGH *(100%) and* *Will freeze*
20 minutes on MEDIUM *(50%)*

100 g (3½ oz) ground almonds
2 tbsp mild curry paste
2 tsp oil
1 medium onion, finely chopped
700 g (1 lb 9 oz) fillet or leg of lamb, cubed
75 ml (2½ fl oz) thick natural yogurt
freshly milled salt and pepper
75 ml (2½ fl oz) double cream
lemon wedges, to serve

1. Mix the almonds and curry paste with 150 ml (¼ pint) water to make a smooth paste.

2. Put the oil and onion in a large bowl, cover and cook for 2 minutes.

3. Add the lamb and stir in the nut paste and yogurt. Season with salt and pepper.

4. Cover and cook for 5 minutes, stirring once or twice. Continue cooking, covered, on MEDIUM (50%) for 20 minutes, stirring occasionally, until the lamb is tender.

5. Stir in the cream and serve with lemon wedges.

KOFTAS IN CURRY SAUCE

Serves 4

Cooking: 12 minutes on HIGH (100%) and
12–15 minutes on MEDIUM (50%)
Will freeze without the yogurt

450 g (1 lb) lean minced lamb
1 medium onion, finely chopped
2 garlic cloves, crushed
2 cm (¾ inch) fresh root ginger, peeled and grated
1 fresh green chilli, seeded and finely chopped
2 tbsp chopped fresh coriander or parsley
1 medium egg, beaten
1 tsp oil
2 tsp ground coriander
1 tsp ground cumin
½ tsp ground turmeric
½ tsp ground cinnamon
300 ml (½ pint) lamb or beef stock
2 tbsp tomato purée
150 ml (¼ pint) natural yogurt

1. Mix together the lamb, half the onion, the garlic, ginger, chilli, herbs and egg. Shape the mixture into 16 small balls (koftas).

2. Arrange the meatballs in a large shallow dish. Cook, uncovered, for 4 minutes, rearranging them once during cooking. Lift them out of the dish and set aside.

3. Put the remaining onion in the dish with the oil. Cover and cook for 2–3 minutes.

4. Stir in the spices, stock and tomato purée. Cover and cook for 5 minutes or until boiling.

5. Add the meatballs (plus their juices) to the dish and coat them with the sauce. Cook, uncovered, on MEDIUM (50%) for 12–15 minutes, rearranging the meatballs once during cooking.

6. Stir in the yogurt before serving.

PORK IN SWEET AND SOUR SAUCE *Serves 4*
Cooking: 15 minutes on HIGH *(100%)* *Will freeze*

227 g can pineapple cubes in fruit juice
chicken or vegetable stock
1 tsp oil
1 medium onion, finely sliced
1 garlic clove, crushed
2 celery sticks, finely sliced
450 g (1 lb) lean pork, finely sliced
2 tbsp tomato purée
3 tbsp red wine vinegar
3 tbsp soy sauce
3 tbsp brown sugar
2 tbsp cornflour
freshly milled salt and pepper
1 green pepper, seeded and finely sliced

1. Drain the pineapple and make up the juice to 300 ml (½ pint) with chicken or vegetable stock.

2. Put the oil, onion, garlic and celery in a large bowl. Cover and cook for 4 minutes, stirring once.

3. Stir in the pork and the pineapple-juice mixture.

4. Whisk together the tomato purée, vinegar, soy sauce, sugar and cornflour, then stir into the pork mixture. Season with salt and pepper.

5. Cover and cook for 5 minutes, stirring once, or until boiling. Continue cooking, covered, for 4 minutes, stirring twice, or until the pork is tender.

6. Stir in the pepper and pineapple, cover and cook for 2 minutes until piping hot.

PORK AND BEAN CASSEROLE   *Serves 4–6*
Cooking: 12 minutes on HIGH *(100%) and*   *Will freeze*
20–30 minutes on MEDIUM *(50%)*

15 g (½ oz) butter
1 tsp oil
1 large onion, finely sliced
700 g (1 lb 9 oz) lean pork, cubed
400 g can chopped tomatoes
1 chicken stock cube
1 tbsp tomato purée
1 tsp dried mixed herbs
freshly milled salt and pepper
415 g can red kidney beans, drained

1. Put the butter, oil and onion in a large bowl, cover and cook for 4 minutes, stirring once.

2. Stir in the pork. Add the remaining ingredients and stir well.

3. Cover and cook for 6–8 minutes, stirring once or twice, or until boiling. Continue cooking, covered, on MEDIUM (50%) for 20–30 minutes, stirring occasionally, until the pork is tender.

CHILLI PORK AND BEANS

Serves 4
Will freeze

Cooking: 14 minutes on HIGH (100%) and 18–20 minutes on MEDIUM (50%)

1 medium onion, finely chopped
1 garlic clove, crushed
450 g (1 lb) pork fillet or tenderloin, thinly sliced
2 tbsp flour
1 tsp chilli powder
½ tsp ground cumin
150 ml (¼ pint) chicken, beef or vegetable stock
400 g can chopped tomatoes
410 g can red kidney beans, drained
freshly milled salt and pepper

1. Put the onion and garlic in a large bowl, cover and cook for 2–3 minutes.

2. Stir in the pork, cover and cook for 3 minutes.

3. Stir in the flour, then add the remaining ingredients.

4. Cover and cook for 6–8 minutes, stirring once or twice, or until boiling. Continue cooking on medium (50%) for 18–20 minutes, stirring occasionally, or until the pork is tender. Remove the lid half way through cooking to reduce and thicken the sauce.

PORK ORIENTAL   *Serves 4*
Cooking: 20 minutes on HIGH *(100%)*   *Will freeze*
plus marinating

2 tbsp soy sauce
1 tbsp Worcestershire sauce
4 tbsp tomato ketchup
1 tbsp brown sugar
1 tbsp coarse-grain mustard
450 g (1 lb) pork fillet or tenderloin, thinly sliced
1 medium onion, thinly sliced
150 ml (¼ pint) chicken or vegetable stock
1 red pepper, seeded and sliced
100 g (3½ oz) mushrooms, thickly sliced

1. Mix together the soy sauce, Worcestershire sauce, ketchup, sugar and mustard. Add the pork and stir to coat it well. Cover and allow to marinate in a cool place for 30 minutes–2 hours.

2. Put the onion in a large bowl, cover and cook for 2–3 minutes.

3. Lift the pork out of its marinade and stir the meat into the onion. Cook, uncovered, for 5–7 minutes, stirring once or twice.

4. Add the marinade and stock. Cook, uncovered, for 5 minutes.

5. Stir in the pepper and mushrooms and cook, uncovered for 4–5 minutes.

SPARE RIBS BARBECUE-STYLE *Serves 4*
Cooking: 10 minutes on HIGH *(100%) and* *Will freeze*
25 minutes on MEDIUM *(50%) plus marinating*

1 small onion, finely chopped
4 tbsp tomato ketchup
4 tbsp Worcestershire sauce
1 tbsp malt vinegar
2 tsp brown sugar
1 tsp mustard powder
½ tsp paprika
900 g (2 lb) small lean pork spare ribs

1. To make the marinade, mix together the onion, ketchup,
   Worcestershire sauce, vinegar, sugar, mustard and paprika.
   Coat the spare ribs with the mixture and arrange them in a
   large shallow dish, pouring over any extra marinade. Cover
   and allow to marinate in a cool place for 1–2 hours.

2. Cover and cook for 10 minutes, then cook on MEDIUM
   (50%) for a further 10 minutes.

3. Arrange the ribs, then cook uncovered on MEDIUM (50%)
   for a further 12–15 minutes, turning them once or twice, or
   until they are tender.

BACON HOTPOT   *Serves 4*

Cooking: about 19 minutes on HIGH *(100%) and*
18 minutes on MEDIUM-LOW *(30%) plus grilling*
Not suitable for freezing

25 g (1 oz) butter
1 medium onion, thinly sliced
225 g (8 oz) carrots, thickly sliced
3 celery sticks, chopped
550 g (1¼ lb) lean unsmoked bacon joint, cubed
2 tbsp flour
300 ml (½ pint) dry cider
1 tbsp coarse-grain mustard
freshly milled salt and pepper
450 g (1 lb) potatoes, thinly sliced

1. Put half the butter in a large flameproof casserole dish with the onion, carrots and celery. Cover and cook for 4 minutes, stirring once.

2. Add the bacon, sprinkle the flour over and stir well. Add the cider, mustard and seasoning.

3. Cover and cook for 8–10 minutes, stirring once or twice, or until boiling.

4. Arrange the potato slices on top, seasoning each layer lightly with salt and pepper. Cover and cook for 5 minutes, then continue cooking on MEDIUM-LOW (30%) for 18 minutes or until the bacon and potatoes are tender.

5. Put the remaining butter in a small bowl and cook for 20 seconds until melted. Brush the melted butter over the potatoes.

6. Put under a hot grill until crisp and golden brown.

AUTUMN BACON CASSEROLE   *Serves 4*
Cooking: 13 minutes on HIGH *(100%) and*   *Will freeze*
25–30 minutes on MEDIUM *(50%)*

1 tbsp butter
12 tiny onions
450 g (1 lb) lean bacon joint, cubed
2 tbsp flour
300 ml (½ pint) bacon, chicken or vegetable stock
2 medium leeks, sliced
1 large carrot, thinly sliced
400 g can tomatoes
50 g (1¾ oz) canned or frozen sweetcorn kernels
freshly milled black pepper

1. Put the butter and onions into a large bowl, cover and cook for 4 minutes, stirring once.

2. Add the bacon and stir in the flour. Gradually stir in the stock, then add the remaining ingredients.

3. Cover and cook for 8–9 minutes, stirring once or twice, or until boiling. Continue cooking, covered, on MEDIUM (50%) for 25–30 minutes, stirring occasionally, until the bacon is tender.

ORANGE-GLAZED GAMMON

Serves 8

Cooking: 15 minutes on HIGH *(100%) and*   *Will freeze*
40–45 minutes on MEDIUM *(50%) plus grilling*

1.4 kg (3 lb) boneless gammon joint
3 tbsp fine-cut orange marmalade
3 tbsp demerara sugar

1. Put the gammon in a large bowl and pour over sufficient boiling water to cover it. Cover and cook for 5 minutes. Allow to stand for 5 minutes, then discard the water.

2. Pour over sufficient boiling water to cover the gammon again. Cover and cook for 10 minutes. Turn the joint over, cover and continue cooking on MEDIUM (50%) for about 40–45 minutes, turning the gammon once, until cooked through.

3. Allow to stand for 10 minutes, then drain off the stock (why not reserve it and make it into a delicious soup?). Cut the skin off the gammon and slash the fat lightly with a sharp knife (a striped or diamond pattern looks good).

4. Mix together the marmalade and sugar and spread the mixture over the fat surface. Cook under a hot grill until golden brown and bubbling hot.

LIVER AND APPLE CASSEROLE *Serves 4*
*Cooking: 9 minutes on HIGH (100%) and
5–8 minutes on MEDIUM (50%)*
Not suitable for freezing

**15 g (½ oz) butter
1 medium onion, thinly sliced
1 medium carrot, thinly sliced
450 g (1 lb) lamb's liver, thinly sliced
2 tbsp flour
freshly milled salt and black pepper
½ tsp dried sage or 1 tsp chopped fresh sage
450 ml (16 fl oz) boiling lamb or beef stock
2 eating apples, cored and sliced**

1. Put the butter, onion and carrot in a large bowl. Cover and cook for 4 minutes, stirring once.

2. Add the liver. Stir in the flour, seasoning and sage. Gradually stir in the boiling stock. Cover and cook for 4–5 minutes or until boiling.

3. Add the apples, cover and cook on MEDIUM (50%) for 5–8 minutes, stirring once, until the liver is just tender.

CHICKEN IN MUSTARD SAUCE

Serves 4

Cooking: 9 minutes on HIGH *(100%) and*
15 minutes on MEDIUM *(50%)*

Will freeze

15 g (½ oz) butter
1 medium onion, sliced
2 medium leeks, sliced
8 chicken thighs skinned
150 ml (¼ pint) chicken stock
150 ml (¼ pint) dry white wine
2 tbsp French mustard
freshly milled salt and pepper
100 g (3½ oz) button mushrooms, sliced

1. Put the butter, onion and leeks in a large bowl. Cover and cook for 4 minutes. Stir well.

2. Arrange the chicken in a circle on top of the vegetables.

3. Mix together the stock, wine, mustard and seasoning. Stir in the mushrooms and pour over the chicken.

4. Cover and cook for 5 minutes, then continue cooking on MEDIUM (50%) for 15 minutes, spooning the sauce over the chicken occasionally during cooking.

CHICKEN IN ORANGE   *Serves 4*
Cooking: 9–14 minutes on HIGH (100%)   *Will freeze*

2 tsp oil
550 g (1¼ lb) boneless chicken breasts, skinned and sliced
2 tsp cornflour
grated rind and juice of 1 large orange
1 chicken or vegetable stock cube
1 tbsp dark soy sauce
1 tbsp clear honey
1 bunch spring onions, sliced
freshly milled salt and pepper
orange slices, to garnish

1. Put the oil and chicken into a medium bowl. Cover and cook for 4–5 minutes, stirring once.

2. Blend the cornflour with the orange juice and the crumbled stock cube. Stir in the orange rind, soy sauce, honey and spring onions. Pour the sauce over the chicken.

3. Cover and cook for 5–9 minutes, stirring occasionally until the sauce thickens and boils and the chicken is tender.

4. Season to taste and serve, garnished with orange slices.

CHICKEN CHASSEUR *Serves 4*
Cooking: 10 minutes on HIGH (100%) and *Will freeze*
20 minutes on MEDIUM (50%)

25 g (1 oz) butter
1 medium onion, finely chopped
2 tbsp flour
150 ml (¼ pint) dry white wine
300 ml (½ pint) boiling chicken stock
freshly milled salt and black pepper
4 chicken breasts, skinned
100 g (3½ oz) button mushrooms
1 tbsp chopped fresh parsley

1. Put the butter and onion in a large bowl, cover and cook for 3 minutes. Stir in the flour, then gradually stir in the wine. Add the boiling chicken stock, salt and pepper. Cook for 3–4 minutes, stirring occasionally, or until the sauce thickens and boils.

2. Add the chicken to the sauce, coating it well. Cover and cook on MEDIUM (50%) for 20 minutes, stirring occasionally, until the chicken is tender.

3. Stir in the mushrooms and parsley, cover and cook for 3 minutes. Allow to stand for 5 minutes before serving.

CURRIED CHICKEN
Cooking: 5 minutes on HIGH *(100%) and*
12–15 minutes on MEDIUM *(50%)*

Serves 4
Will freeze

2 tsp oil
1 large onion, finely chopped
2 garlic cloves, crushed
4 boneless chicken breasts, skinned and thickly sliced
2 tbsp curry paste
2 tsp flour
1 tbsp white wine vinegar
juice of 1 lemon
150 ml (¼ pint) chicken stock
cooked rice, poppadoms (see page 97) and
   mango chutney, to serve

1. Put the oil, onion and garlic into a medium bowl, cover and cook for 2–3 minutes.

2. Stir in the chicken, cover and cook for 2 minutes.

3. Blend the curry paste with the flour, vinegar and lemon juice. Stir into the stock and pour over the chicken.

4. Cover and cook on MEDIUM (50%) for about 12–15 minutes, stirring occasionally, or until the chicken is tender. Serve with rice, poppadoms and mango chutney.

ORIENTAL CHICKEN   *Serves 4*
Cooking: 10–12 minutes on HIGH (100%)
Not suitable for freezing

2 tsp oil
4 boneless chicken breasts, skinned and thinly sliced
1 tbsp grated fresh root ginger
2 tbsp soy sauce
2 tbsp dry sherry
1 bunch spring onions, sliced
2 red or yellow peppers (or one of each), seeded and
  thinly sliced
225 g can water chestnuts, drained and sliced
2 tbsp toasted sesame seeds
few drops sesame oil

1. Put the oil and chicken in a large bowl and mix well. Cover
   and cook for 4 minutes, stirring once.

2. Mix together the ginger, soy sauce and sherry and add to
   the bowl with the onions, peppers and water chestnuts.

3. Cover and cook for 6–8 minutes, stirring occasionally,
   until the chicken is cooked through.

4. Stir in the sesame seeds and sesame oil before serving.

TURKEY IN TOMATO SAUCE WITH MUSHROOMS

Cooking: 24–29 minutes on HIGH (100%)   *Serves 4*
Will freeze

3 tbsp flour
freshly milled salt and pepper
700 g (1 lb 9 oz) boneless turkey fillet, cubed
25 g (1 oz) butter
1 large onion, finely chopped
1 garlic clove, crushed
150 ml (¼ pint) chicken stock
150 ml (¼ pint) dry white vermouth
400 g can chopped tomatoes
225 g (8 oz) button mushrooms
2 tbsp chopped parsley

1. Season the flour with salt and pepper. Add the turkey and toss to coat it well.

2. Put the butter, onion and garlic into a large bowl. Cover and cook for 4 minutes, stirring once.

3. Add the turkey to the onion mixture and stir in the stock, vermouth and tomatoes. Cover and cook for 12–15 minutes, stirring once.

4. Stir in the mushrooms and cook, uncovered, for 8–10 minutes or until the turkey is tender and the sauce has reduced slightly. Add the parsley just before serving.

11

EGGS AND CHEESE

Tips for cooking eggs

- Don't cook a whole egg (in its shell) unless you have a special gadget for 'boiling' eggs in the microwave. Without one, steam builds up inside the egg, increasing the pressure until the egg explodes; this can happen even after the microwave is switched off. An egg-boiling gadget encloses the egg in metal so that the microwaves can't reach it; it is the heat from the water and the surrounding metal that cooks the egg.

- Eggs at room temperature produce the best results.

- Prick the yolks of eggs that are to be left whole during cooking (e.g. baked and poached eggs) to prevent them from bursting open.

- Overcooking makes eggs tough so stop cooking just before they are fully cooked; they will finish cooking during a short standing time.

- Eggs cooked on HIGH (100%) often cook too quickly. Results vary depending on your microwave but you may get better results on MEDIUM (50%).

Tips for cooking cheese

• Add cheese to a dish towards the end of cooking when possible, to prevent it overcooking and becoming stringy.

• Cheese melts quickly and evenly if it is grated rather than sliced or diced.

• If cheese cooks too quickly on HIGH (100%), better results rnay be achieved by using MEDIUM (50%) power.

BAKED EGGS

1. Break the eggs into small cups, dishes or ramekins. Prick the yolks. Arrange the dishes in a circle in the microwave.

2. Cook on MEDIUM (50%) until almost set:
   1 egg – about 1 minute
   2 eggs – about 1½ minutes
   3 eggs – about 2 minutes
   4 eggs – about 2½ minutes

3. Allow to stand for 1–2 minutes before serving.

POACHED EGG

1. Pour 150 ml (¼ pint) water into a medium bowl or jug. Add a dash of vinegar. Bring to the boil.

2. Break an egg into the boiling water. Prick the yolk.

3. Cook for ½–1 minute.

4. Allow to stand for 1–2 minutes before lifting out with a slotted spoon and serving.

SCRAMBLED EGGS   *Serves 2*
Cooking: 1 minute 20 seconds–2 minutes on HIGH *(100%)*
Not suitable for freezing

4 medium eggs
4 tbsp milk
25 g (1 oz) butter
freshly milled salt and pepper

1. In a medium bowl or jug, beat together the eggs and milk. Add the butter and season to taste.

2. Cook for 1 minute 20 seconds–2 minutes, stirring or whisking frequently (each time the egg sets around the edges of the bowl). Stop cooking when the eggs are still slightly undercooked – they will continue cooking as they are being served.

Note: If you find the eggs cook too quickly on HIGH (100%), reduce the power to MEDIUM (50%).

PIPERADE   *Serves 2*
Cooking: about 6 minutes on HIGH (100%)
Not suitable for freezing

25 g (1 oz) butter
1 small onion, finely chopped
1 garlic clove, crushed
1 medium green pepper, seeded and thinly sliced
227 g can chopped tomatoes, drained
freshly milled salt and black pepper
4 medium eggs, beaten

1. Put the butter, onion, garlic and pepper in a medium bowl. Cover and cook for 2½ minutes.

2. Stir in the tomatoes and season to taste with salt and pepper. Cook, uncovered, for 40 seconds.

3. Stir in the eggs and cook, uncovered for 1½–3 minutes, stirring frequently, until the eggs are lightly scrambled.

BACON AND MUSHROOM OMELETTE   *Serves 2*

Cooking: 7 minutes on HIGH (100%)
Not suitable for freezing

15 g (½ oz) butter
2 lean bacon rashers, chopped
50 g (1¼ oz) button mushrooms, thinly sliced
2 spring onions, chopped
4 medium eggs, beaten
freshly milled salt and pepper

1. Put the butter and bacon in a shallow dish measuring about 20 cm (8 inch) in diameter. Cook, uncovered, for 2 minutes.

2. Stir in the mushrooms and onions and cook, uncovered, for 1 minute.

3. Season the eggs with salt and pepper and pour them over the bacon mixture. Cook, uncovered, for 3–4 minutes, until just set, lifting the cooked areas from the sides of the dish after each minute to allow the liquid to run to the edges. Cut into wedges to serve.

EGG AND CHEESE ROLL   *Serves 1*
Cooking: 1½–2 minutes on HIGH (100%)
Not suitable for freezing

1 soft bread roll
15 g (½ oz) butter
1 medium egg
25 g (1 oz) grated cheese

1. Cut a slice off the top of the bread roll and reserve. Scoop out the crumbs from the centre of the roll.

2. Put the butter in a small bowl and cook for 30 seconds until melted. Brush some butter in the cavity of the roll. Brush the remainder over the cut side of the reserved slice.

3. Break the egg into the roll and prick the yolk. Sprinkle with grated cheese and replace the lid.

4. Cook, uncovered, for 1½–2 minutes, or until the egg is just set. Serve hot or cold.

CHEDDAR FONDUE   *Serves 4–6*
Cooking: 6–8 minutes on HIGH *(100%)*
Not suitable for freezing

1 garlic clove, halved
450 g (1 lb) mature Cheddar cheese, grated
1 tbsp cornflour
300 ml (½ pint) white wine
1 tsp lemon juice
25 g (1 oz) butter
freshly milled pepper
pinch of ground nutmeg
crusty bread cubes, to serve

1. Rub the inside of a large bowl with the cut sides of the garlic.

2. Add the cheese and cornflour to the bowl and mix well. Stir in the wine, lemon juice and butter.

3. Cook, uncovered, for 6–8 minutes, stirring frequently, until the cheese melts and the mixture is thick and smooth.

4. Season with pepper and stir in the nutmeg. Serve with bread cubes – spear them on long forks and dip into the fondue.

EGGS FLORENTINE *Serves 4*

Cooking: 10 minutes on HIGH (100%) and
4 minutes on MEDIUM (50%) plus grilling
Not suitable for freezing

700 g (1 lb 9 oz) fresh spinach, chopped
25 g (1 oz) butter
3 tbsp flour
300 ml (½ pint) milk
75 g (2¾ oz) mature Cheddar cheese, grated
freshly milled salt and pepper
4 medium eggs

1. Put the spinach in a large bowl, cover and cook for 5 minutes, stirring once, or until just tender. Drain well.

2. Put the butter, flour and milk in a medium bowl or jug and whisk well. Cook for about 5 minutes, whisking frequently, until the sauce thickens and boils. Stir in the cheese and season with salt and pepper.

3. Break the eggs into four small dishes or ramekins and prick the yolks. Cook on MEDIUM (50%) for 3–4 minutes, until the egg whites are just set.

4. Put the spinach in a shallow flameproof dish. Slide the eggs out of their dishes onto the spinach. Pour the cheese sauce over and brown under a hot grill.

12

VEGETABLES

Fresh vegetables cooked in the microwave are simply delicious. Because they are cooked quickly and in the minimum amount of liquid, they retain their full flavour and colour, and cook to the stage where they are still slightly crunchy. Small quantities of vegetables are very successful too, cooked in a small dish so there is no saucepan to wash up. Cooked vegetables also reheat well in the microwave – to look and taste as if they had only just been cooked.

Tips for cooking vegetables

- Use good quality vegetables for best results. Old, tired vegetables will toughen and dry out.

- Choose even-sized vegetables for cooking whole. Otherwise, cut them into even-sized pieces to encourage even cooking.

- Prick the skins of whole vegetables in several places before cooking, to prevent them bursting open.

- Frozen vegetables can be cooked straight from the freezer.

- Arrange whole vegetables in a circle, to encourage them to cook evenly. Avoid putting one in the centre.

- When cooking more than 450 g (1 lb) cut vegetables, best results may be obtained if they are cooked in batches.

- Add 3–4 tbsp water to the vegetables. Root vegetables and old vegetables often need more. Extra water may also be needed if you want to cook vegetables until they are very soft.

- Season vegetables with salt after cooking or they will become dry and tough.

- Cook most vegetables on HIGH (100%). If they tend to overcook or shrivel, it may be preferable to cook on a slightly lower power, such as MEDIUM-HIGH (75%).

- Cover cut vegetables during cooking to keep the moisture in.

- Stir, shake or turn vegetables occasionally to encourage them to cook evenly.

- Cooking times will depend on the type and quantity of vegetables as well as their age. As a guide, 450g (1 lb) cut vegetables take 6–10 minutes. Always underestimate the time and test in the usual way – by inserting the tip of a knife.

- Whole vegetables, such as potatoes, need to stand for several minutes before serving, to allow the temperature to even out.

BLANCHING VEGETABLES

1. Put up to 450g (1 lb) prepared vegetables in a bowl with 3–4 tbsp water.

2. Cover and cook for 3–4 minutes, stirring once, until the vegetables are hot.

3. Drain and tip the vegetables into ice-cold water. Drain them again, then put into polythene bags and freeze.

JACKET POTATOES

1. Scrub and dry potatoes weighing about 175 g (6 oz) each. Using a fork, prick their skins in several places. Put them in the microwave, in a circle.

2. Cook, uncovered, until tender:
   4-6 minutes for 1
   7–9 minutes for 2
   8–12 minutes for 3
   10–15 minutes for 4.
   Turn them over at least once during cooking.

3. Allow the potatoes to stand for 5 minutes before serving.

CARROTS IN ORANGE GLAZE   *Serves 4*
Cooking: 10 minutes on HIGH *(100%)*
Not suitable for freezing

450 g (1 lb) carrots, thinly sliced
25 g (1 oz) butter
5 tbsp orange juice
1 tsp clear honey
freshly milled salt and black pepper
1 tbsp chopped fresh parsley

1. Put the carrots in a large bowl and add the butter, orange juice and honey. Cover and cook for about 8–10 minutes, stirring occasionally, until the carrots are tender.

2. Season to taste and stir in the parsley.

LEEKS PARMESAN   *Serves 4*
Cooking: 13 minutes on HIGH *(100%)*
Will freeze – best without the breadcrumbs and cheese

50 g (1¾ oz) butter
50 g (1¾ oz) fresh breadcrumbs
25 g (1 oz) Parmesan cheese, finely grated
2–3 medium leeks, about 450 g (1 lb) thinly sliced
1 tsp soft brown sugar
2 tbsp double cream
freshly milled salt and black pepper

1. Put 25 g (1 oz) butter in a shallow heatproof container and cook for 20 seconds or until melted. Stir in the breadcrumbs, coating them well. Cook, uncovered, for about 2–3 minutes, stirring every minute, until golden brown. Add the cheese.

2. Put the remaining butter, leeks and sugar in a bowl. Cover and cook for about 6–8 minutes, stirring occasionally, until the leeks are just tender.

3. Stir in the cream and season to taste. Cook for 1 minute.

4. Tip the leeks and their sauce into a flameproof dish and scatter the breadcrumb mixture over the top. If wished, brown under a hot grill for a few minutes before serving.

PARSLEY BAKED ONIONS *Serves 4*
Cooking: 10–12 minutes on HIGH *(100%)*
Not suitable for freezing

350 g (12 oz) small or pickling onions, peeled
1 tsp lemon juice or white wine vinegar
25 g (1 oz) butter
3 tbsp chopped fresh parsley
freshly milled salt and black pepper

1. Put all the ingredients in a medium bowl, cover and cook for 10–12 minutes, stirring occasionally.

2. Allow to stand for 5 minutes before serving.

POTATOES DAUPHINOIS   *Serves 4*

Cooking: 5 minutes on HIGH *(100%) and*
25 minutes on MEDIUM *(50%) plus grilling*
Not suitable for freezing

700 g (1 lb 9 oz) potatoes, thinly sliced
50 g (1¾ oz) Cheddar or Gruyère cheese, grated
freshly milled salt and black pepper
150 ml (¼ pint) double cream
150 ml (¼ pint) milk
1 garlic clove crushed
pinch of ground nutmeg
15 g (½ oz) butter

1. Butter a flameproof dish. Layer the potatoes with the cheese in the dish, seasoning each layer lightly.

2. Mix the cream with the milk and add the garlic and nutmeg. Pour evenly over the potatoes. Dot with the butter.

3. Cover and cook for 5 minutes.

4. Uncover and cook on MEDIUM (50%) for about 20–25 minutes until the potatoes are tender.

5. Brown under a hot grill.

BEETROOT AND APPLE SALAD *Serves 4*
Cooking: 15 minutes on HIGH (100%) *Will freeze*

225 g (8 oz) beetroot, peeled and diced
2 tbsp red wine vinegar
1 tsp sugar
2 celery sticks, thinly sliced
1 large eating apple, cored and diced

1. Put the beetroot, vinegar and sugar in a bowl with 4 tbsp water. Cover and cook for about 15 minutes, stirring, occasionally, or until the beetroot is tender.

2. Stir in the celery and apples. Serve warm or chilled.

GINGERED CABBAGE   *Serves 4*
Cooking: 9½ minutes on HIGH (100%)
Not suitable for freezing

40 g (1½ oz) butter
1 tbsp grated fresh root ginger
1 small clove, crushed
450 g (1 lb) cabbage, shredded
freshly milled salt and black pepper

1. Put the butter in a large bowl and cook for 20 seconds or until melted.

2. Stir in the ginger and garlic. Add the cabbage and stir well to coat it with the butter.

3. Cover and cook for about 7–9 minutes, stirring occasionally, or until tender.

4. Season to taste before serving.

VEGETABLES IN CREAM SAUCE

Serves 2 as a main meal, 4 as an accompaniment
Cooking: 10 minutes on HIGH (100%)
Not suitable for freezing

25 g (1 oz) butter
1 large onion, thinly sliced
4 medium carrots, thinly sliced
4 celery sticks, thinly sliced
225 g (8 oz) small broccoli florets
100 g (3½ oz) button mushrooms
150 ml (¼ pint) vegetable stock
1 tbsp cornflour
150 ml (¼ pint) soured cream
freshly milled salt and black pepper
1 tbsp chopped fresh chives
50 g (1¾ oz) toasted cashew nuts or pine nuts

1. Put the butter and onion in a large bowl, cover and cook for 2 minutes.

2. Stir in the carrots, celery, broccoli, mushrooms and stock. Cover and cook for about 6 minutes, stirring occasionally, until the vegetables are just tender.

3. Mix the cornflour with the cream to make a smooth paste, season to taste and add the chives. Stir into the vegetables. Cook, uncovered, for about 2 minutes, stirring once, until the sauce thickens and boils.

4. Scatter the nuts over the top and serve immediately.

RATATOUILLE   *Serves 6*
Cooking: 13 minutes on HIGH *(100%) and*   *Will freeze*
15 minutes on MEDIUM *(50%)*

1 medium aubergine, sliced
salt
2 tbsp olive oil
1 large onion, thinly sliced
1 large garlic clove, crushed
2 large courgettes, sliced
1 red pepper, seeded and sliced
1 yellow pepper, seeded and sliced
400 g can chopped tomatoes
2 tbsp chopped fresh herbs, such as thyme, basil
   and/or parsley
2 tbsp tomato purée
freshly milled salt and black pepper

1. Sprinkle the aubergine slices with salt, if wished, and allow to stand for 30 minutes. Rinse and dry well.

2. Put the oil, onion and garlic in a large bowl. Cover and cook for 3 minutes.

3. Stir in the aubergine slices, courgettes and peppers. Cover and cook for 5 minutes, stirring once.

4. Add the tomatoes, herbs and tomato purée. Season well. Cover and cook for 5 minutes, then continue cooking on MEDIUM (50%) for 15 minutes, stirring gently occasionally.

5. Allow to stand for at least 10 minutes before serving hot or cold.

MIXED BEAN MEDLEY   *Serves 4–6*
Cooking: 7 minutes on HIGH (100%) and   *Will freeze*
10 minutes on MEDIUM (50%)

2 tbsp olive oil
1 large onion, thinly sliced
2 garlic cloves, crushed
1 tbsp tomato purée
3 tbsp chopped fresh herbs, such as thyme, oregano,
   and/or fennel
1 tsp sugar
227 g can chopped tomatoes
grated rind and juice of 1 lemon
410 g can haricot beans, drained
410 g can red kidney beans, drained
freshly milled salt and black pepper
salad and garlic bread, to serve

1. Put the oil, onion and garlic in a large bowl, cover and cook
   for 2–3 minutes.

2. Mix together the tomato purée, herbs, sugar, tomatoes,
   lemon rind and juice. Pour the sauce over the onion, cover
   and cook for 4 minutes, stirring once, or until boiling.

3. Stir in the beans and season to taste. Cover and cook on
   MEDIUM (50%) for 10 minutes.

4. Serve hot or at room temperature with salad and garlic
   bread.

CURRIED VEGETABLES

Cooking: 19 minutes on HIGH *(100%)*

Serves 4
Will freeze

2 tbsp oil
2 tsp ground coriander
1 tsp ground cumin
½ tsp turmeric
½ tsp chilli powder
1 medium onion, finely chopped
2 garlic cloves, crushed
2 medium potatoes, chopped
2 medium carrots, sliced
1 small cauliflower, cut into small florets
227 g can tomatoes
150 ml (¼ pint) vegetable stock
2 courgettes, thickly sliced
2 tbsp coconut cream
freshly milled salt and black pepper
150 ml (¼ pint) natural yogurt
cooked rice, to serve

1. Put the oil, spices, onion and garlic in a large bowl, cover and cook for 1–2 minutes, stirring once.

2. Add the potatoes, carrots and cauliflower. Stir well to coat them with the spices.

3. Mix the tomatoes with the vegetable stock and add to the bowl.

4. Cover and cook for 10–12 minutes, occasionally stirring gently.

5. Add the courgettes and coconut cream, cover and cook for 5 minutes, stirring once or twice, until the vegetables are tender.

6. Season to taste, stir in the yogurt and serve with rice.

14

RICE, PASTA, PULSES
AND CEREALS

The cooking of rice, pasta and pulses is not necessarily quicker in a microwave. However, microwaving is certainly a convenient and clean method.

Instant breakfast cereals and porridge are quick and convenient too, particularly when individual portions are prepared in the microwave.

Tips for cooking rice, pasta and pulses
- Use a large deep bowl, to allow the contents to boil up.

- Adding a little oil to the cooking water helps to prevent it from boiling over.

- Large quantities, over 450 g (1 lb), are best cooked conventionally on the hob.

- Always add boiling water to the rice, pasta or pulses. Boil the water in a kettle to save time.

- Salt can be added to the cooking water of pasta. Rice and pulses are best seasoned with salt after cooking, to prevent them from toughening.

- Though covering during cooking keeps moisture in, results are just as good if no cover is used – and there is less chance of the contents boiling over and flooding the floor of the microwave.

- Stir well after adding the boiling water, before cooking.

- Rice need not be stirred again, but pasta and pulses should be stirred occasionally during cooking.

- Allow a standing time of 5 minutes before serving.

RICE – Basic method
1. Put the rice in a large deep bowl. Pour over boiling water:
       300 ml (½ pint) for 100 g (3½ oz) white rice
       450 ml (16 fl oz) for 100 g (3½ oz) brown rice
       600 ml (1 pint) for 225 g (8 oz) white rice
       700 ml (1¼ pints) for 225 g (8 oz) brown rice.

2. Stir well. Cook for about 10 minutes for white rice, or 20–30 minutes for brown rice, until the rice is tender and has absorbed all the water.

3. Season to taste, stir, cover and allow the rice to stand for 5 minutes before serving.

PASTA – Basic method

1. Put the pasta in a large deep bowl with salt and a little oil, if wished. Pour over sufficient boiling water to cover the pasta by at least 2.5 cm (1 inch). Stir well.

2. Cook for:
    3–4 minutes for 225 g (8 oz) fresh pasta
    7–10 minutes for 225 g (8 oz) dried pasta
    10–14 minutes for 450 g (1 lb) dried pasta.

2. Stir occasionally during cooking, to prevent the pasta pieces sticking together. Stop cooking when the pasta is still slightly undercooked.

3. Stir well, cover and allow to stand for 5 minutes before draining and serving.

PULSES – Basic method

1. Soak 225 g (8 oz) pulses in plenty of cold water overnight. Alternatively, pour plenty of boiling water over the pulses, cover and allow to stand for 1–2 hours. (Split peas and lentils do not need soaking before cooking.)

2. Drain and put the pulses into a large bowl and pour over enough boiling water to cover them by at least 2.5 cm (1 inch).

3. Cook on HIGH (100%), stirring occasionally, until tender. Always use HIGH (100%) as the water must boil when cooking pulses.

> *Aduki beans:* 30–35 minutes
> *Black-eye beans:* 25–35 minutes
> *Cannellini beans:* 30–45 minutes
> *Chick peas:* 50–60 minutes
> *Flageolet beans:* 35–45 minutes
> *Haricot beans:* 25–35 minutes
> *Lentils:* 20–30 minutes
> *Mung beans:* 20–30 minutes
> *Peas:* 30–45 minutes
> *Red kidney beans:* 30–45 minutes
> *Split peas:* 20–30 minutes

4. Cover and allow to stand for 5 minutes before draining and using.

PORRIDGE *Serves 2*

Cooking: 4–6 minutes on MEDIUM *(50%)*
Not suitable for freezing

50 g (1¼ oz) porridge oats
300 ml (½ pint) milk
salt, sugar, or honey

1. Put the oats in a medium bowl and add the milk. Cook, uncovered, for about 4–6 minutes on MEDIUM (50%) or until the porridge thickens and boils, stirring frequently.

2. Add salt, sugar or honey to taste.

MACARONI CHEESE   *Serves 4*
Cooking: 14 minutes on HIGH (100%)   *Will freeze*
plus grilling

225 g (8 oz) macaroni
40 g (1½ oz) butter
40 g (1½ oz) flour
½ tsp mustard powder
600 ml (1 pint) milk
175 g (6 oz) Cheddar cheese, grated
freshly milled salt and black pepper

1. Put the macaroni in a large bowl and pour over enough
   boiling water to cover it by 2.5 cm (1 inch). Stir well.
   Cook, uncovered, for 8 minutes, stirring occasionally.
   Allow to stand.

2. Meanwhile, put the butter, flour, mustard powder and milk
   into a medium bowl or jug and whisk well. Cook for about
   6 minutes, whisking frequently, until the sauce thickens
   and boils. Stir in 100 g (3½ oz) cheese and season to taste
   with salt and pepper.

3. Drain the macaroni and stir it into the sauce. Pour the
   mixture into a flameproof dish and sprinkle with the
   remaining cheese.

4. Brown under a hot grill.

VEGETABLE RISOTTO   *Serves 4*
Cooking: 21–24 minutes on HIGH (100%)
Not suitable for freezing

1 tbsp oil
25 g (1 oz) butter
1 large leek, finely sliced
1 garlic clove, crushed
175 g (6 oz) arborio or risotto rice
600 ml (1 pint) vegetable stock
150 ml (¼ pint) dry white vermouth
225 g (8 oz) small broccoli florets
225 g (8 oz) button mushrooms
grated Parmesan cheese, to serve

1. Put the oil, butter, leek and garlic in a large bowl, cover
   and cook for 3–4 minutes.

2. Stir in the rice, cover and cook for 2 minutes.

3. Add the stock and vermouth. Cook, uncovered, for 10
   minutes.

4. Stir in the broccoli and mushrooms and cook, uncovered,
   for 6–8 minutes.

5. Cover and allow to stand for 5 minutes. Serve, sprinkled
   with Parmesan cheese.

TURKEY PILAFF   *Serves 4*
Cooking: 24 minutes on HIGH *(100%)*
Not suitable for freezing

25 g (1 oz) butter
50 g (1¾ oz) flaked almonds
2 tsp oil
1 medium onion, finely sliced
100 g (3½ oz) button mushrooms
225 g (8 oz) long grain rice
600 ml (1 pint) boiling chicken stock
25 g (1 oz) raisins
4 turkey breast fillets

1. Put the butter in a shallow heatproof dish and cook for 20
   seconds until melted. Add the almonds and cook for 2–3
   minutes, stirring frequently, until golden brown. Drain on
   kitchen paper.

2. Pour any excess butter from the almonds into a large bowl.
   Add the oil, onion and mushrooms, cover and cook for 2–3
   minutes.

3. Stir in the rice and cook for 2 minutes.

4. Add the boiling stock and raisins. Add the turkey, pushing
   the pieces under the surface of the stock.

5. Cover and cook for 10 minutes, stirring occasionally.
   Uncover and cook for a further 5 minutes until the turkey
   is cooked through.

6. Scatter the almonds over the top to serve.

BULGUR WHEAT SALAD

Serves 4–6

Cooking: 5 minutes on HIGH *(100%)*
Not suitable for freezing

225 g (8 oz) bulgur wheat
600 ml (1 pint) boiling vegetable stock
2 tbsp olive oil
grated rind and juice of 1 small lemon
1 bunch spring onions, thinly sliced
half a cucumber, diced
4 tomatoes, skinned and chopped
4 tbsp chopped fresh mint
4 tbsp chopped fresh parsley
freshly milled salt and black pepper
10 black olives, pitted
fresh crusty bread, to serve

1. Put the bulgur wheat in a large bowl, stir in the boiling stock, cover and cook for 5 minutes. Allow to stand, covered, for 15 minutes.

2. Add the oil, lemon rind and juice, onions, cucumber, tomatoes, mint and parsley. Season to taste with salt and pepper. Gently stir the mixture until well mixed, then tip it into a large serving bowl.

3. Halve the olives and scatter over the salad. Serve at room temperature with crusty bread.

LASAGNE   *Serves 4*
Cooking: 24 minutes on HIGH *(100%) and*   *Will freeze*
20 minutes on MEDIUM *(50%) plus grilling*

1 tsp oil
1 medium onion, finely chopped
1 garlic clove, crushed
350 g (12 oz) lean minced beef
1 beef stock cube
1 tbsp chopped fresh oregano
2 tbsp tomato purée
400 g can chopped tomatoes
freshly milled salt and black pepper
25 g (1 oz) butter
25 g (1 oz) plain flour
300 ml (½ pint) milk
100 g (3½ oz) mature Cheddar cheese, grated
6 sheets fresh lasagne
25 g (1 oz) Parmesan cheese, grated

1. Put the oil, onion and garlic in a large bowl, cover and cook for 2–3 minutes, stirring once.

2. Crumble the beef and add to the bowl. Cover and cook for 5 minutes, stirring twice.

3. Crumble in the beef stock cube. Add the oregano, tomato purée, tomatoes and seasoning. Cover and cook for 12 minutes, stirring occasionally.

4. Put the butter, flour and milk in a bowl or jug, and whisk. Cook, uncovered, for about 4 minutes, whisking frequently, until the sauce thickens and boils. Add the Cheddar cheese.

5. Grease a shallow rectangular flameproof dish. Put half of the lasagne sheets in the bottom. Cover them with half of

the meat sauce then half of the cheese sauce. Repeat these layers and scatter the Parmesan cheese over the top.

6. Cover and cook on MEDIUM (50%) for about 20 minutes until the pasta is tender.

7. Brown the top of the lasagne under a hot grill.

14

FRUIT AND DESSERTS

Fruit is perfect for cooking in the microwave, staying in shape and retaining all its juice, flavour and colour. Light sponge and suet puddings are cooked in minutes instead of taking hours of steaming on the hob. Crumbles, cheesecakes, milk puddings and egg custard are all ideal candidates for microwave cooking too, and don't forget to use the microwave to dissolve gelatine and to melt chocolate for mousses and other desserts.

Tips for cooking fruit
- Pierce or split the skins of whole fruits, such as apples, to prevent them bursting open.
- Frozen fruit can be cooked straight from the freezer.
- Add water to hard fruits and fruits with skins, such as apples and plums. 3–4 tbsp is a good guide.

- Soft fruits, such as raspberries and blackcurrants; fruits with a high water content, such as rhubarb; and apple slices for a purée, usually need no additional liquid.

- Either dissolve sugar in the cooking liquid, or add sugar after cooking. Do not sprinkle sugar over fruits with skins, such as plums or blackcurrants, or the skins will toughen.

- Cover during cooking, to keep the moisture in and to help the fruit cook evenly.

- Most fruit can be cooked on HIGH (100%), but if it tends to overcook or burst open, try lowering the power to MEDIUM (50%). The difference in the cooking time will be minimal.

- Cooking times depend on the type, quantity and age of the fruit. As a guide:

- 450 g (1 lb) soft fruit takes 2–5 minutes

- 450 g (1 lb) hard fruit takes 7–10 minutes.

- Stir gently or reposition whole fruit occasionally during cooking.

- Allow to stand for 3–5 minutes before serving.

Tips for cooking sponge and suet puddings
When cooking a conventional recipe in the microwave, add extra liquid to the mixture. About 1 tbsp per egg is a good guide.

- Use a pudding bowl which is large enough to allow the pudding to rise up.

- A transparent bowl allows you to see when the pudding is cooked.

- Lightly grease the bowl before adding the pudding mixture.

- Cover the pudding loosely with a 'hat' of greaseproof or non-stick paper, to keep moisture in and to allow the pudding to rise above the top of the bowl if necessary.

- Stand the bowl on a microwave rack or an upturned saucer, to encourage even cooking.

- Cook on HIGH (100%) for 3–7 minutes, depending on the size of pudding.

- Stop cooking when the surface of the pudding is still slightly moist, but the mixture beneath it is cooked. The surface will dry as the pudding stands.

- Allow to stand for 3–5 minutes before turning the pudding out, to let it settle.

- Turn the pudding on to a warmed plate.

- If the bottom of the pudding is still slightly undercooked, do not put it back into its bowl. Put the plated pudding back into the microwave and cook briefly until set.

- **Tips for cooking milk puddings**
- Use a large deep bowl, to allow the pudding to boil up.

- Cook, uncovered, on HIGH (100%) until the mixture boils, then continue cooking on MEDIUM (50%) or MEDIUM-LOW (30%) until the pudding is cooked:
  semolina, tapioca and ground rice take about 10 minutes
  whole rice takes 30–40 minutes.

- Stir occasionally during cooking.

BAKED APPLES   *Serves 4*
Cooking: 5–7 minutes on HIGH *(100%)*
Not suitable for freezing

4 cooking apples, each weighing about 225–275 g
   (8–9½ oz), cored
6–8 tbsp mincemeat

1. Using a small sharp knife, make a shallow cut through the skin around the middle of each apple.

2. Arrange the apples in a shallow container and add 2 tbsp water. Cover and cook for 3 minutes.

3. Fill the apple centres with mincemeat. Cover and cook for 2–4 minutes until the apples are tender. Should any of the apples cook too fast and threaten to burst open, you may prefer to reduce the microwave power level to MEDIUM (50%) and continue cooking until the apples are tender.

PEARS IN CIDER   *Serves 4*
Cooking: 11 minutes on HIGH *(100%)*
Not suitable for freezing

4 pears, peeled
300 ml (½ pint) sweet cider
2 tbsp demerara sugar
½ tsp almond essence

1. Arrange the pears, sitting them upright, around the edge of a shallow dish. Add the cider and sugar.

2. Cover and cook for about 6–8 minutes until the pears are tender but not collapsing, spooning the juice over them occasionally during cooking. Carefully lift the pears on to a serving dish.

3. Return the juices to the microwave and cook, uncovered, for 2–3 minutes until slightly reduced. Add the almond essence and serve the sauce with the pears. Serve hot or chilled.

HONEY-BAKED BANANAS   *Serves 4*
Cooking: 6 minutes on HIGH *(100%)*
Not suitable for freezing

25 g (1 oz) butter
juice of 1 medium orange
1 tbsp clear honey
4 medium bananas
whipped cream or ice cream to serve

1. Put the butter, orange juice and honey in a shallow dish. Cook for 1–2 minutes until the butter has melted. Stir well.

2. Skin the bananas and halve them lengthways. Add to the dish, turning to coat them well with the butter mixture.

3. Cook for 3–4 minutes until the bananas just begin to bubble. Serve with whipped cream or ice cream.

APPLE AND BLACKBERRY CRUMBLE   *Serves 4*
Cooking: 10 minutes on HIGH *(100%)*
Not suitable for freezing

450 g (1 lb) cooking apples, peeled, cored and sliced
2 tbsp sugar
225 g (8 oz) fresh or frozen blackberries
75 g (2¾ oz) soft butter
175 g (6 oz) plain flour
75 g (2¾ oz) demerara sugar

1. Put the apples and sugar in a 20 cm (8 inch) soufflé dish with 1 tbsp water. Cover and cook for 3 minutes. Stir in the blackberries.

2. Rub the butter into the flour until the mixture resembles fine breadcrumbs. Stir in the sugar. Tip the mixture on top of the fruit and level the surface.

3. Cook, uncovered, for about 6–7 minutes. Allow to stand for a few minutes before serving.

RICE PUDDING *Serves 4*

Cooking: 7 minutes on HIGH *(100%) and*
30–40 minutes on MEDIUM-LOW *(30%) plus*
grilling, if wished
Not suitable for freezing

50 g (1¾ oz) pudding rice
600 ml (1 pint) milk
25 g (1 oz) sugar
ground nutmeg
1 tbsp butter

1. Put the rice, milk and sugar into a large bowl. Sprinkle with nutmeg and add the butter.

2. Cook for about 7 minutes, stirring twice, or until boiling. Cover and cook on MEDIUM-LOW (30%) for 30–40 minutes, stirring occasionally, until thick and creamy.

3. If wished, pour the pudding into a flameproof dish and brown lightly under a hot grill.

EGG CUSTARD   *Serves 4*
Cooking: 15–20 minutes on MEDIUM *(50%)*
Not suitable for freezing

3 eggs
600 ml (1 pint) milk
25 g (1 oz) caster sugar
ground nutmeg

1. Lightly beat the eggs, then gradually beat in the milk.
   Strain the mixture into a dish*, then stir in the sugar and
   sprinkle with nutmeg.

2. Stand the dish in a larger container with sufficient boiling
   water to come half way up the dish.

3. Cook, uncovered, on MEDIUM (50%) for 15–20 minutes
   until just set. Allow to stand for 5 minutes before serving.

*Alternatively cook the custard in four individual soufflé or
ramekin dishes and serve chilled.

APRICOT UPSIDE DOWN PUDDING   *Serves 6*
Cooking: 11 minutes on MEDIUM-HIGH *(75%)*   *Will freeze*

410 g can apricot halves in fruit juice
25 g (1 oz) soft butter
25 g (1 oz) soft brown sugar
150 g (5½ oz) butter
150 g (5½ oz) caster sugar
2 medium eggs, beaten
175 g (6 oz) self-raising flour, sieved

1. Drain the apricots, reserving 5 tbsp of the juice.

2. Put the butter in a 20 cm (8 inch) soufflé dish and cook for 30 seconds or until melted. Brush the base and sides of the dish with the butter, then scatter the brown sugar on to the buttered surface. Arrange the apricots, cut side upwards, in the base of the dish.

3. Cream the margarine and caster sugar together until light and fluffy. Add the eggs, a little at a time, beating well after each addition. Fold in the flour and the reserved fruit juice.

4. Spread the pudding mixture over the apricots and level the surface.

5. Place the dish on a microwave rack or upturned saucer and cook, uncovered, for about 10 minutes until the surface is still slightly moist but the pudding beneath it is cooked.

6. Allow to stand for 5 minutes before turning out on to a warmed plate.

SYRUP SPONGE PUDDING   *Serves 4*
Cooking: 6 minutes on HIGH (100%)   *Will freeze*

2 tbsp golden syrup
50 g (1¾ oz) butter
50 g (1¾ oz) caster sugar
1 medium egg, beaten
100 g (3½ oz) self-raising flour
few drops of vanilla extract
3 tbsp milk

1. Butter a 600 ml (1 pint) pudding basin and put the syrup in the bottom.

2. Put the butter, sugar, egg, flour and vanilla extract in a bowl and beat well until smooth. Gradually stir in the milk. Spoon the mixture on top of the syrup and level the surface.

3. Cover loosely with a 'hat' of greaseproof paper and place the pudding on a microwave rack or upturned saucer. Cook for about 6 minutes until the surface is still slightly moist but the pudding beneath it is cooked. Allow to stand for 5 minutes before turning out on to a warmed plate.

BLACKCURRANT CHEESECAKE *Serves 6*
Cooking: 30 seconds on HIGH *(100%) and* *Will freeze*
8 minutes on MEDIUM *(50%) plus cooling*

You need a blender or food processor for this recipe.

50 g (1¼ oz) butter
100 g (3½ oz) digestive biscuits, crushed
175 g (6 oz) soft cream cheese
100 g (3½ oz) cottage cheese
2 medium eggs, beaten
2 tbsp caster sugar
1 tsp cornflour
410 g can blackcurrant pie filling or conserve

1. Lightly grease an 18 cm (7 inch) flan dish.

2. Put the butter in a bowl and cook for 30 seconds until melted. Add the biscuits and stir well. Press the mixture into the base of the flan dish.

3. Put the cream cheese, cottage cheese, eggs, sugar and cornflour into a blender or processor and purée until smooth. Pour on to the biscuit base.

4. Cook, uncovered, on MEDIUM (50%) for about 8 minutes or until set (don't worry if the centre is still slightly moist – this will set as the cheesecake cools).

5. Allow to cool before spreading the pie filling over the top of the cheesecake.

WHITE CHOCOLATE MOUSSE

Serves 4–6

Cooking: 3–4 minutes on MEDIUM-LOW   *Will freeze*
(30%) and 45 seconds on HIGH *(100%)*

175 g (6 oz) white chocolate
1 tbsp clear honey
1 tsp gelatine
150 ml (¼ pint) whipping cream
2 medium egg whites
pinch salt
25 g (1 oz) white or plain chocolate, to decorate

1. Break the white chocolate into a bowl. Add 3 tbsp water and the honey. Cook on MEDIUM-LOW (30%) for about 3–4 minutes. Stir well until melted and smooth.

2. Put 3 tbsp water in a small bowl and sprinkle the gelatine over. Allow it to stand for 1 minute. Cook on HIGH (100%) for 30–45 seconds, stirring every 15 seconds, until clear (make sure it does not boil). Stir into the white chocolate.

3. Whip the cream until it stands in soft peaks. Fold it into the chocolate mixture.

4. Using a clean bowl and whisk, whisk the egg whites with the salt until stiff. Fold into the chocolate mixture. Spoon into 4–6 small glasses and chill until set.

5. To decorate, chill the remaining chocolate, then make chocolate shavings by drawing a potato peeler across it. Sprinkle some on to the top of each mousse.

CHOCOLATE MOUSSE   *Serves 4*
Cooking: 3–4 minutes on MEDIUM *(50%)*   *Will freeze*
plus chilling

225 g (8 oz) plain chocolate
40 g (1½ oz) butter
4 medium eggs, separated
4 tsp rum
whipped cream and grated chocolate, to decorate

1. Break the chocolate into a bowl and add the butter. Cook on MEDIUM (50%) for about 3–4 minutes, stirring occasionally, until melted.

2. Beat in the egg yolks and rum. Whisk the egg whites until stiff and fold them into the chocolate mixture.

3. Spoon into 4 serving dishes or glasses and chill for about 2 hours until set. Decorate with whipped cream and grated chocolate to serve.

APPLE AND SPICE CAKE – see page 172.

15

CAKES, BISCUITS AND SWEETS

Cakes cooked in the microwave rise well and their flavour is good. Their texture is slightly pudding-like and they do not brown and crisp as when baked in a traditional oven. Generally, very moist mixtures are suited to microwave cooking, as are recipes in which the fats and sugars are melted together. The microwave recipes in this section have been tried and tested over the years.

Some biscuit recipes can be microwaved but because they can only be cooked in small batches, and need frequent attention, it is more convenient to cook them conventionally. However, shortbread and flapjacks are successful and I have included the recipes for these, together with microwave meringues.

Lastly, the microwave makes speedy work of melting

butter, chocolate, and so on, for sweets – a few recipes are included.

Tips for making cakes

• Choose circular dishes with vertical sides. Ring moulds produce the most successful cakes, with no chance of the centre remaining uncooked.

• When trying a recipe for the first time, choose a deep container – cakes rise considerably during cooking. Half fill it only.

• Lightly grease the cooking container. Do not coat it with flour or a disagreeable crust will form on the outside of the cake.

• Line the base of the container with non-stick baking paper or greased greaseproof paper, for easy removal of the cake.

• When cooking a conventional recipe in the microwave, add extra liquid to the mixture – about 1 tbsp per egg is a good guide. Fruit cakes should have a very soft dropping consistency (see page 171).

• Plump up dried fruit before adding it to a cake mixture (see method on page 171).

• Sugar must be well blended into the mixture – lumps of sugar attract microwaves and burn easily.

• Small cakes should be arranged in a circle in the microwave, with the centre left free.

• Place the dish on a microwave rack to make sure the cake cooks evenly.

• Cook sponge-type cakes on HIGH (100%) and fruit cakes on

MEDIUM (50%) or MEDIUM-LOW (30%). Check with your oven manufacturer's instruction book too.

- Stop cooking when the surface of the cake is still slightly moist but the mixture beneath it is cooked. The sauce will dry out as it stands.

- Allow a standing time before turning the cake out – 5 minutes for sponge-type cakes and 20 minutes for fruit cakes.

- Turn the cake out on to a cooling rack lined with non-stick baking paper – to prevent it sticking to the rack.

CHOCOLATE CAKE *Serves 6–8*
Cooking: 4–4½ minutes on HIGH (100%) *Will freeze*
Not suitable for freezing

200 g (7 oz) self-raising flour
1 tsp baking powder
½ tsp bicarbonate of soda
2 tbsp cocoa powder
75 g (2¾ oz) caster sugar
2 medium eggs, beaten
150 ml (¼ pint) corn or sunflower oil
150 ml (¼ pint) milk
2 tbsp golden syrup

1. Grease a 20 cm (8 inch) cake or soufflé dish and line its base with a circle of non-stick baking paper.

2. Sieve the flour, baking powder, bicarbonate of soda and cocoa into a medium bowl. Stir in the sugar.

3. Whisk together the eggs, oil, milk and syrup. Add to the dry ingredients and beat well until smooth. Pour the mixture into the prepared dish.

4. Place the dish on a microwave rack or upturned saucer. Cook for 4–4½ minutes until the surface is still slightly moist but the cake beneath it is cooked. Allow to stand for 10 minutes before turning the cake out on to a cooling rack lined with non-stick baking paper.

LEMON SPONGE RING

Cooking: 5½ minutes on HIGH *(100%)*

Serves 8
Will freeze

150 g (5½ oz) caster sugar, plus extra for coating
175 g (6 oz) self-raising flour
1 tsp baking powder
175 g (6 oz) soft margarine
3 medium eggs, beaten
2 tbsp lemon curd

Topping:
4 tbsp lemon juice
3 tbsp caster sugar
crystallised lemon slices

1. Grease a medium ring mould and lightly coat the greased surface with the extra caster sugar.

2. Sieve the flour with the baking powder.

3. Cream the margarine and 150 g (5½ oz) caster sugar together until light and fluffy. Add the eggs, a little at a time, beating well after each addition. Fold in the flour mixture.

4. Put the lemon curd into a small bowl and cook for 30 seconds until melted. Stir into the cake mixture with 2 tbsp warm water. Pour into the prepared ring mould.

5. Cook for about 4–5 minutes or until the surface is still slightly moist but the cake beneath it is cooked. Allow to stand for 2–3 minutes before turning the cake out on to a cooling rack lined with non-stick baking paper.

6. To make the topping, mix the lemon juice with the caster sugar and pour over the warm cake. Decorate with lemon slices and allow to cool.

FRUIT CAKE RING   *Serves 16*
Cooking: 3 minutes on HIGH (100%) and   *Will freeze*
30–40 minutes on MEDIUM-LOW (30%)

500 g (1 lb 2 oz) mixed dried fruit
150 ml (¼ pint) orange or apple juice
250 g (9 oz) plain flour
1 tsp mixed spice
1 tsp ground ginger
1 tsp ground nutmeg
175 g (6 oz) butter, softened
175 g (6 oz) soft dark brown sugar
4 medium eggs
2 tbsp black treacle
50 g (1¾ oz) walnuts, chopped
100 g (3½ oz) glacé cherries, chopped
3 tbsp milk

1. Grease a 2 litre (3½ pint) ring mould and line its base with non-stick baking paper.

2. Put the fruit and orange or apple juice in a bowl, cover and cook for 3 minutes until plumped up and soft.

3. Sieve the flour with the spice, ginger and nutmeg. Cream the butter and sugar together until light and fluffy. Add the eggs, one at a time, adding 1 tbsp flour with each one. Add the remaining ingredients and stir in the warm fruit and juice to make a very soft dropping consistency.

4. Pour the mixture into the prepared mould and level the surface.

5. Cook, uncovered, on MEDIUM-LOW (30%) for 30–40 minutes until a wooden cocktail stick, inserted in the cake, comes out clean.

6. Allow to stand for 20 minutes, then turn out on to a cooling rack lined with non-stick baking paper. Strip off the paper and allow the cake to cool (any moisture on the surface will dry as it cools).

APPLE AND SPICE CAKE   *Serves 16*
Cooking: 10–12 minutes on MEDIUM-HIGH *(50%)*
Will freeze

450 g (1 lb) eating apples, peeled, cored and finely chopped
100 g (3½ oz) plain white flour
100 g (3½ oz) plain wholemeal flour
2 tsp baking powder
1½ tsp mixed spice
175 g (6 oz) soft brown sugar
100 g (3½ oz) butter, softened
2 medium eggs
6 tbsp milk
sifted icing sugar, to serve

1. Grease a 1.7 litre (3 pint) ring mould and line the base with non-stick baking paper. Arrange one-third of the apple on top of the paper.

2. Put the white and wholemeal flours, baking powder, spice, sugar, margarine, eggs and milk into a large bowl and beat until smooth.

3. Fold in the remaining apple.

4. Spoon the mixture into the ring mould and level the top.

5. Cook, uncovered, for 10–12 minutes until the surface is still slightly moist but the cake beneath it is cooked. Allow to stand for 15 minutes, then turn the cake out onto a plate. Dust with icing sugar to serve. Delicious served warm.

ALMOND SLICES   *Makes 6*
Cooking: 3 minutes on HIGH *(100%)*   *Will freeze*

100 g (3½ oz) soft margarine
75 g (2¾ oz) clear honey
1 medium egg, beaten
75 g (2¾ oz) plain flour, sifted
75 g (2¾ oz) ground almonds
25 g (1 oz) flaked almonds, toasted
sifted icing sugar, to serve

1. Lightly grease a 20 cm (8 inch) flan dish and line the base with non-stick paper.

2. Cream the margarine and honey until light and fluffy. Beat in the egg, then fold in the flour and ground almonds.

3. Tip the mixture into the prepared dish and level the top. Sprinkle the flaked almonds over the top. Place the dish on a microwave rack or upturned saucer and cook, uncovered, for about 3 minutes until firm.

4. Allow to stand for 5 minutes in the dish, then turn out onto a cooling rack. Allow to cool completely before cutting into wedges.

5. Dust with icing sugar to serve.

CORNFLAKE CRISPIES   *Makes 12*
Cooking: 2½–3½ minutes on MEDIUM *(50%)*
Not suitable for freezing

225 g (8 oz) plain chocolate
50 g (1¾ oz) butter
1 tbsp golden syrup
50 g (1¾ oz) cornflakes

1. Break the chocolate into a medium bowl and add the butter and syrup. Cook on MEDIUM (50%) for 2½–3½ minutes, stirring frequently, until melted.

2. Fold in the cornflakes.

3. Put spoonfuls into paper cake cases and chill until set.

MICROWAVE MERINGUES   *Makes about 24*
Cooking: 1–2 minutes on HIGH *(100%)*
Not suitable for freezing

1 medium egg white
275–350 g (9½–12 oz) icing sugar
whipped cream, to serve

1. Lightly whisk the egg white to break it up. Sieve the icing sugar to remove all lumps. Line the microwave turntable, or a large heatproof plate, with non-stick baking paper.

2. Beat the icing sugar into the egg white, a little at a time, until you have a firm fondant-like paste.

3. Divide the mixture into small balls and arrange eight at a time, in a circle, on the baking paper. Cook, uncovered, for 1–2 minutes until risen and firm to the touch (take care not to overcook them).

4. Allow them to cool before carefully lifting them off the paper. Serve with whipped cream.

SHORTBREAD

Makes 6–8 wedges
Will freeze

Cooking: 8–9 minutes on MEDIUM *(50%)*

115 g (4 oz) butter, softened
50 g (1¾ oz) caster sugar, plus extra for sprinkling
150 g (5½ oz) plain flour
25 g (1 oz) semolina

1. Grease an 18 cm (7 inch) flan dish or plate and line the base with non-stick baking paper.

2. Cream the butter and sugar together until light and fluffy.

3. Sieve the flour and semolina. Fold them into the mixture, then lightly knead it to form a dough.

4. Press the dough into the dish or plate and level the surface. Prick well with a fork. Cook for 8–9 minutes or until set.

5. Allow to stand for 10 minutes, then mark into wedges and sprinkle with extra caster sugar. Cool completely before lifting them off the paper.

CHOCOLATE BISCUIT BISCUITS   *Makes 10*
Cooking: 1–2 minutes on MEDIUM *(50%)*
Not suitable for freezing

100 g (3½ oz) plain chocolate
100 g (3½ oz) butter
1 tbsp clear honey
2 tbsp double cream
100 g (3½ oz) digestive biscuits, crumbled
50 g (1¾ oz) chopped nuts
25 g (1 oz) ready-to-eat dried apricots, finely chopped
25g (1 oz) glacé cherries, chopped

1. Lightly grease a 20 cm (8 inch) flan dish and line the base with non-stick baking paper.

2. Break the chocolate into a large bowl. Cut the butter into cubes and add to the chocolate with the honey. Cook on MEDIUM (50%) for about 1–2 minutes, stirring frequently, until melted.

3. Stir in the remaining ingredients.

4. Tip the mixture into the prepared dish and level the top. Chill until just set, mark into 10 wedges, then chill until firm.

FLAPJACKS   *Makes 16*
Cooking: 3–5 minutes on HIGH (100%)   *Will freeze*

75 g (2¾ oz) butter
50 g (1¾ oz) soft brown sugar
2 tbsp golden syrup
175 g (6 oz) porridge oats

1. Grease a shallow 12 × 23 cm (5 × 9 inch) dish.

2. Put the butter, sugar and syrup in a bowl and cook for 1–2 minutes, stirring once, until the sugar has dissolved. Stir well, then add the oats. Stir well again.

3. Tip the mixture into the dish and press it in well. Stand the dish on a microwave rack or upturned saucer and cook for 2–3 minutes until firm to touch.

4. Allow to cool slightly before marking into 16 pieces. Cool completely before turning out of the dish.

WHITE CHOCOLATE CLUSTERS   *Makes 12 sweets*
Cooking: 1–2 minutes on HIGH *(100%) and*
2–3 minutes on MEDIUM-LOW *(30%)*
Not suitable for freezing

40 g (1½ oz) flaked almonds
75 g (2¾ oz) white chocolate
25 g (1 oz) crystallised ginger, finely chopped
25 g (1 oz) ready-to-eat dried apricots, finely chopped

1. Put the almonds in a shallow heatproof dish and cook for 1–2 minutes, stirring frequently, until lightly browned.

2. Break the chocolate into a bowl and cook on MEDIUM-LOW (30%) for about 2–3 minutes, stirring occasionally, until melted. Stir in the almonds, ginger and apricots.

3. Put small spoonfuls of the mixture into paper sweet cases and chill until firm.

ALMOND AND COCONUT FUDGE   *Makes 16 slices*
Cooking: 1 minute on HIGH (100%) plus chilling
Will freeze

50 g (1¾ oz) plain chocolate
50 g (1¾ oz) unsalted butter
50 g (1¾ oz) dark brown sugar
1 tbsp milk
25 g (1 oz) ground almonds
50 g (1¾ oz) macaroons, crushed
25 g (1 oz) desiccated coconut
icing sugar

1. Break the chocolate into a bowl and add the butter, sugar and milk. Cook for about 1 minute, stirring once or twice, until melted.

2. Stir in the almonds, macaroons and coconut. Cover and refrigerate for about 30 minutes or until the mixture is firm enough to handle.

3. Tip the mixture on to a sheet of non-stick baking paper or greaseproof paper and shape it into a sausage about 23 cm (9 inch) long. Wrap it well, twisting the ends like a Christmas cracker. Chill for 1 hour or more.

4. Remove the paper, sieve some icing sugar over the edge and cut it into 1 cm (½ inch) slices.

MUESLI BITES   *Makes about 28*
Cooking: 1–2 minutes on MEDIUM *(50%)*
Not suitable for freezing

100 g (3½ oz) plain chocolate
50 g (1¾ oz) butter
50 g (1¾ oz) golden syrup
225 g (8 oz) breakfast muesli

1. Break the chocolate into a bowl and add the butter and syrup. Cook on MEDIUM (50%) for about 1–2 minutes, stirring frequently, until melted.

2. Stir in the muesli.

3. Put small spoonfuls of the mixture into paper sweet cases and allow to cool until set.

CHOCOLATE TRUFFLES

Makes about 24

Cooking: 2–3 minutes on MEDIUM *(50%)*   *Will freeze*
plus 30 minutes cooling and firming time

100 g (3½ oz) plain chocolate
50 g (1¼ oz) butter
100 g (3½ oz) trifle sponges
25 g (1 oz) icing sugar
1 tbsp brandy or rum
cocoa powder, icing sugar or chocolate vermicelli

1. Break the chocolate into a bowl and add the butter. Cook on MEDIUM (50%) for 2–3 minutes, stirring frequently, until melted.

2. Finely crumble the sponges and sieve the sugar. Stir the sponge crumbs, sugar and brandy or rum into the chocolate.

3. Allow to cool for about 30 minutes until firm enough to handle. Shape into small balls and coat them with sifted cocoa powder or icing sugar or chocolate vermicelli. Refrigerate until firm.

16

. . . AND DON'T FORGET

Bread
Warm fresh bread or freshen up stale bread in your microwave.
Whole loaves, rolls or slices should be heated for seconds on
MEDIUM (50%) or MEDIUM-LOW (30%) until warmed through.

Butter
Soften butter for spreading or baking. 100 g (3½ oz) takes
about 15 seconds on MEDIUM-LOW (30%).

Chocolate
To melt chocolate, break it into a bowl and cook on MEDIUM
(50%) or MEDIUM-LOW (30%), stirring frequently, until
melted, this will take seconds. Do not overheat it.

Drinks
The microwave is ideal for heating individual drinks, so long
as these basic rules are followed:

- Use a large cup or mug with sloping sides (that is, the top is
  wider than the bottom).

- Stir the drink before putting it into the microwave and
  occasionally during heating.

- Do not heat milk in its milk bottle.

- Do not heat water in a teapot.

Gelatine

To dissolve gelatine, choose one of the following methods:

1. Sprinkle it on to water, or some of the liquid from the recipe, and allow to stand for 1 minute. Heat, stirring every 15–20 seconds, until the gelatine has dissolved. Do not boil.

2. Heat some of the liquid from the ingredients until it is very hot, but not quite boiling. Quickly add the gelatine, stirring briskly until dissolved.

Herbs

Many fresh herbs can be dried in the microwave. Small-leaf or chopped herbs work best. Chopped chives, mint and sage are suitable; leaves of thyme and rosemary are good too. Basil is not so successful because it burns easily and loses its flavour (it is best frozen). Parsley also tends to lose its flavour.

Arrange the washed and dried leaves (or chopped herbs) in a shallow even layer on kitchen paper (not recycled paper – it may burn). Heat on MEDIUM (50%), stirring or repositioning frequently and checking every 10–20 seconds or so, until the herbs are dry and will crumble when rubbed between your fingers. Allow to stand for 10 minutes before storing in airtight containers.

Jam

Melt jam to spread on cakes. Heat it carefully or it will become too hot and could burn.

Jelly

Save time by melting jelly cubes in the microwave. Break the jelly into a bowl or jug and add 150 ml (¼ pint) water. Cook for about 1 minute until melted. Stir well and top up the jelly with cold water.

Oranges and lemons
Squeeze extra juice from oranges and lemons after warming them in the microwave first. Heat them for 1 minute.

Preserves
Small batches of jams, jellies, marmalades and chutneys are very successful in the microwave.

INDEX

Also in the Right Way series

THE COMBINATION MICROWAVE COOK
by Annette Yates and Caroline Young

This book is specifically written for cooks who use a combination microwave oven or a microwave with a built-in grill. The 100+ recipes – from simple snacks, vegetable, meat and poultry dishes to sweet and savoury bakes and pastries – have all been developed to make full use of these ultra-modern appliances.

* Revised and updated edition with brand-new recipes
* Easy-to-follow step-by-step methods
* Packed with useful tips and delicious serving suggestions for 2 or 4 people

Create crisp, flaky pastry, golden-brown gratin and baked pasta dishes, main dishes, cakes and desserts, all cooked (and browned) in a fraction of the conventional cooking time.

MICROWAVE RECIPES FOR ONE
by Annette Yates

Delicious recipes for the person who lives alone, or who has to prepare individual meals for some other reason: perhaps members of the family need to eat at different times or have conflicting tastes and preferences, or perhaps someone is on a special diet which requires food to be cooked separately.

There are recipes for: breakfasts; soups, starters and sauces; fish, meat, poultry, vegetable, cheese, egg and pasta dishes; and desserts – PLUS an indispensable cooking guide which explains how to adapt family recipe instructions to the smaller amounts needed for a single portion.

www.constablerobinson.com/rightway

Three ways to order *Right Way* books:

1. Visit www.constablerobinson.com and order through our website.

2. Telephone the TBS order line on **01206 255 800**.
   Order lines are open Monday – Friday, 8:30am–5:30pm.

3. Use this order form and send a cheque made payable to TBS Ltd or
   charge my ☐ Visa ☐ Mastercard ☐ Maestro (issue no. _____)

Card number:_____

Expiry date: _____ Last three digits on back of card:_____

Signature: _____

(your signature is essential when paying by credit or debit card)

No. of copies	Title	Price	Total
	The Combination Microwave Cook	£5.99	
	Microwave Recipes for One	£4.99	
	For P&P add £2.75 for the first book, 60p for each additional book		
	Grand Total		£

Name: _____

Address:_____

_____ Postcode: _____

Daytime Tel. No./Email _____
(in case of query)

**Please return forms to Cash Sales/Direct Mail Dept.,
The Book Service, Colchester Road, Frating Green,
Colchester CO7 7DW.**

Enquiries to readers@constablerobinson.com.

Constable and Robinson Ltd (directly or via its agents)
may mail, email or phone you about promotions or products.

☐ Tick box if you do not want these from us ☐ or our subsidiaries.

www.constablerobinson.com/rightway